WOMEN OF BABALON

A Howling of Women's Voices

Linda Falorio ✦ Charlotte Rodgers ✦ Mishlen Linden
Lou Hotchkiss Knives ✦ Emma Doeve
Diane Narraway ✦ Geraldine Lambert
Semirani Vine ✦ Lorraine Sherwin
Dianne Mystérieux ✦ Lilith Dorsey
Ayahna Kumarroy ✦ Madeleine Ledespencer
Maegdlyn Morris ✦ Sarah-Jayne Farrer
Sharmon Davidson-Jennings

Edited by Mishlen Linden

BLACK MOON PUBLISHING
CINCINNATI, OHIO
USA

Black Moon Manifesto

It is the Will and mission of Bate Cabal/Black Moon to effectively manifest unique and insightful occult Works for the esoteric community in a manner that is unfettered by commercial considerations.

© Copyright 2019 Black Moon Publishing, LLC
All rights reserved.

Cover painting "Blood Moon" by Sharmon Davidson-Jennings

BlackMoonPublishing.com

Design and layout by
Jo Bounds of Black Moon Publishing, LLC

ISBN: 978-1-890399-63-4

United States • United Kingdom • Europe • Australia • India

First there was Nothing.
Then Nothing splintered into bits.
Earth, Water, Fire and Air took their stations
And from this rose Babalon.
Keeper of Life, Creatrix of all
Eternally growing, eternally present,
With the Gods She coupled.
Hence the Spirits were formed.
Who would deny this?

This publication offers honor and respect to all of the elders, the crones, the women who have come before and paved the way. We thank Nema (Maggie) for being among the first to challenge assumptions about "What happens when Babalon gets old?"
Through you we thank them all.

--- CONTENTS ---

Blood Rites of Babalon by Linda Falorio 7
Qulielfi: From *The Shadow Tarot* – Art by Linda Falorio 21
Characith: From *The Shadow Tarot* – Art by Linda Falorio 22
Hemethterith: From *The Shadow Tarot* – Art by Linda Falorio ... 29
Strange Birth – Art by Emma Doeve 30
A Darker Magick by Emma Doeve 31
At the Heart of the Labyrinth – Art by Emma Doeve 37
Mistress of Eros – Art by Emma Doeve 38
The Dæmon Lover by Emma Doeve 39
Gestation – Art by Sharmon Davidson-Jennings 48
Lucifer's Lover by Diane Narraway 49
In Honor of the Lightbearers – Art by Geraldine Lambert 65
Lucifers Child – Art by Semirani Vine 69
Babalon and the Beast – Poem and Art by Lorraine Sherwin 72
Sexual Magick: Point to Point by Charlotte Rodgers 73
Lilith – Art by Mishlen Linden 78
In the Garden of Earthly Delights:
    From the Magickal Record of Mishlen Linden 79

Babalon – Art by Dianne Mystérieux 120
Watch Her Wrap Her Legs Around This World:
    Babalon, Sex, Death, Conception, Punk Rock
    and the Mysteries by Lou Hotchkiss Knives 121
Untitled – Art by Ayahna Kumarroy 154
Sex and Possession/Voodoo Love
    The Gede We Always Knew Was There by Lilith Dorsey 155
And you shall see the shades which she becomes –
    Art by Madeleine Ledespencer 158
The Warrior Babalon by Maegdlyn Morris 159
A Love Letter by Sarah-Jayne Farrer 167
Chant d'Automne – Art by Sarah-Jayne Farrer................. 168
Spirit House/Womb: A Place for Things to Grow –
Art by Mishlen Linden....................................169
Glaistig – Art by Lorraine Sherwin 170
Glaistig by Sarah-Jayne Farrer 171
Notes on Glaistig – From Wikipedia 172
Outro by Lou Hotchkiss Knives 173
En Finale by Mishlen Linden 178
Biographies 179
Babalon Community Contacts 190
Nuit – Art by Mishlen Linden 191

Blood Rites of Babalon

by Linda Falorio

There is a uniqueness in the sexuality of those born into a female body. There is blood and the frisson of death that sits astride us that can only be experienced by those born into a female form in part due to the ever-constant danger and delight in the possibility of pregnancy resulting from the rites themselves. These are deeply felt gifts of the great goddess that thread their way through our mitochondrial DNA, passed down to us through countless generations of our grandmothers.

The world is a much different place than it was years ago when I was first formed, and concepts that were once daring are now rather pedestrian and mundane. However, the practices I describe are clearly not for everyone. I have provided here a series of techniques and practices to assure safety on these funambulatory pathways as I share with you my personal reflections on the tantric path of the Blood Rites of Babalon.

Women of Babalon, this one's for you. Men, read on if you want to know our deepest secrets.

The Path of Babalon

To walk the path of Babalon is to allow oneself the freedom of a passionate existence. This passionate path is not an easy path for women and those who dare it are often frowned upon with disapproval

and even, in times past, burning at the stake or stoning, or shameful public branding with the demeaning "Scarlet Letter." Let me explain. What I mean by "passionate existence" is to allow oneself to experience pure sensation as the world presents itself to us, to suspend value judgments and move beyond the perceived polarities of pleasure-pain, good-evil, attraction-repulsion by which we commonly limit and define our everyday human lives.

As an "experiment," if only for a moment, allow yourself to totally yield to sensations of pleasure and desire in encountering all facets of existence, without fear of dissolution of the "I." Yield to desire, yet retain your personal integrity, independence and power. Once able to open heightened sensitivities to an awareness of existence as pure sensation, we are able to stand-in for the goddess and channel transpersonal love and acceptance for all things in creation, regardless of perceived beauty or ugliness, attractiveness or repugnance, gender, age, or personal emotional reactions.

Five Techniques for Encountering the Other, For Encountering the Self

1. Take what they give.

No matter what your personal reaction might normally be, whether fear, attraction, boredom, even repulsion, accept the person before you without judgment. In each encounter in your daily life, take what others give you. If there is anger, accept that. If there is sadness, allow sadness to pass into your consciousness. If there is sexual attraction, allow that attraction into your energy field. Absorb these energies into yourself through touching the other lightly on the shoulder, take their hand in yours, and let essence flow from their eyes into yours. Radiate back to them your acceptance.

2. Imagine having sex with everyone you encounter.

Whether you find the other attractive or not, whether old or young, regardless of traditional sexual taboos, imagine having sex with everyone you encounter as an extension of technique 1. Continue this practice until you are able to imagine sexual encounters without excitement, repulsion, guilt, shame or fear. Once all such emotions have lost their power over you, you will have developed kindness and tolerance for others' differentness, for we love that best which is most like ourselves.

3. Dissolve ego-boundaries through the moment of "the kiss."

In the ineffable moment of a kiss, the boundaries between oneself and the other blur. Prolong this moment until you feel an energy and awareness other than "yourself" move through you. Work gradually. Kiss a plant. Kiss an inanimate object, a stone, a car, a pencil, your athamé. Kiss an animal, your cat, your dog, kiss a frog, a butterfly. Kiss another person. For that moment of the kiss, merge with and learn something of the being of the other. Take their energies fully into your being, savor them, roll them around in your mind. Allow the kiss to last longer than is ordinary for a kiss. Break away from the kiss and gaze into the other's eyes for as long as they will allow.

4. The other as a mirror: Trading places.

Gaze into the eyes of another person and through active imagination "become" that person looking back at you. Become "the other." Ask permission before attempting this technique as the experience can be very intense, even unsettling for both parties. When successful there is a flash of union, a flow of pure energy, a reaching out and identification with the other and you will see yourself through the eyes of another. This may be pleasant or extremely unpleasant. For the adventurous, try this with someone you do not like, or with whom you are angry. Expect some surprising results.

5. The Magick Mirror.

Gaze at your own reflection in a mirror until it is no longer familiar to you, until the face in the mirror has become that of an alien other gazing back at you. Radiate kindness to the person that you find now in the mirror gazing back at you. Give her your acceptance. Allow your love to flow out to her and then return from the other in the mirror as it is reflected back to you.

Preparing the Astral Temple - Green Elephants!

Before creating the astral temple both in waking and in dreams, Banish. Banish. Banish. Do not under any circumstances, whatever you do, think at any time of green elephants. Of course, it is relatively easy to "banish" but the secret of any banishing is to "not think of green elephants" at the crucial moment. Therefore, drill the following rites until you can literally do them with your eyes closed, do them in your sleep, do them in your dreams and on the astral and never ever think of green elephants.

1. Light a single candle in a dark room. Seated in your meditation pose, gaze at the candle flame for 1 minute. Close your eyes and focus your intention on the after-image of the flame. Strive to keep the image of the flame centered, vivid and stable, reignite the flame as it begins to fade.

2. Visualize each of five tatwa images one at a time until you are able to keep each image vibrant and stable. The tatwa images to use are a red triangle, a yellow square, a purple sphere, a white crescent, and a black oval. To help with this visualization, you can use the after-image as you did with the practice of the candle flame. Make a set of flash cards with the colors reversed so that they will create an after image on your

retina of the correct color that you can then use as your focus. Make a green triangle on a red ground, a purple square on a yellow ground, a yellow sphere on a purple ground, a black crescent on a white ground and a white oval on a black ground. Gaze at each image for one minute, then close your eyes and focus on the after image created on your retina that will be of the correct color for each tatwa. Keep the image vivid, stable and alive for as long as possible. Do this first with your eyes closed, and then with your eyes open.

3. Now with the power of your creative imagination, draw a pentagram of blue light beginning at the lower left point, one line at a time. Keep the image of the pentagram stable and bright for as long as you are able. With the power of your creative imagination, inscribe an inverted pentagram of light in red, first with your eyes closed and then with your eyes open. "See" the pentagram thus created as stable, solid, and superimposed upon your physical surroundings. Pointing with your athamé, now draw the 7-rayed Star of Babalon in red astral light, first with eyes closed and then eyes open. Keep the image vibrant and alive with light, superimposed upon physical reality for as long as possible.

4. Practice the "Star Ruby" banishing ritual until you can perform it in your sleep and on the astral on demand, all the way through without becoming lost or distracted. (Note: The pentagrams can be drawn upright in blue light, or reversed in red, depending on the direness, or not, of your current situation.)

Note: Demons really take notice when you banish using Greek!

Face East, making the Sign of Silence.
Now make the sign of the cross as you Will, hissing: "Soi, Kteis, Ischros, Ucharistos."

Throw your arms into a victorious "V," shouting: "IOA!"

Using both hands, hurl a pentagram of light from your forehead, hissing: "Therion!"

Drawing a circle of light while turning to the North: Hurl a pentagram of light hissing: "Nuit!"

Continuing the circle of light while turning to the West: Hurl a pentagram of light hissing: "Babalon!"

Continuing the circle of light while turning to the South: Hurl a pentagram of light hissing: "Hadit!"

Standing in the center of the circle of protection you have just created, facing East, perform the signs of N.O.X. *"Vir, Mulier, Puer, Puella."*

Extending arms in the form of a Tau, hiss in a low guttural voice: "Before me shrieking, behind me the ultimate end of Chaos, on my right hand, on my left hand, stream forth cursing demons. Oh that around me flame the pentagrams and in the stele the star of six must stand!"

Make the sign of the cross to close the rite as you Will, hissing: "Soi, Kteis, Ischros, Ucharistos."

Throw your arms into a victorious "V," shouting: "IOA!"

Return to the Sign of Silence.

Using your athamé, sword or wand, draw a pentagram of light horizontally, topmost point outward across each window-sill and each door-frame to seal each door and window, every ingress or egress to the sacred space you have created, including fireplaces and chimneys.

5. Call the Guardians of the quarters to cleanse and protect your sacred

space: Facing East, strongly visualize the Angels of the quarters as you call them each by name in a loud, clear and commanding voice: "Before me Raphael, behind me Gabriel, to my left hand Ariel, to my right hand Michael. Around me flame the pentagrams, above me shines the six-rayed star."

6. Visualize the Angels growing to fill the space into which you have called them, no matter how large that space may be, as they spread their auras to form a protective sphere around you. Now visualize your body wrapping with white astral light, beginning from back to front, from your feet up over your head and down again. Now wrap the astral light counter-clockwise from your left foot around and around your body to the top of you head, resting consciousness in the crown chakra and allowing healing energy to both fill and cleanse your aura. (Note: you can perform this for someone who is ill and in need of healing.)

7. Having wrapped the body with light, establish a breathing rhythm. Visualize the life force around you as brilliant dancing points of light. Breathe light into your body; allow yourself to experience the surrounding ocean of vibrating energy in which we constantly swim and from which we derive our being. As the breathing rhythm becomes established and you move deeper and deeper into a meditative state, your consciousness calms, becoming lucid and clear.

8. Visualize energy and light pulling through the bones of your legs with each breath. Now breathe light and energy through the bones of your arms. Breathe light and energy through the pores of your skin, until your body feels cleansed, alive and open to sensation. Breathe energy up from the base of your spine to the top of your skull and then breathe that energy back down from your head to the base of

your spine, filling your body with energy and light as you breathe the energy current up and down your spine, awakening the sleeping serpent, Kundalini to ready yourself for the next stages of your tantric practice.

9. Breathe energy up and out through the top of your head, then down and around your body, until the brilliant blue light of your protective aura grows and fills the circle that encloses you within your sacred space, becoming brighter, more vital with each breath. Now breathe through the top of the skull until your mind expands and opens to the universe of Stars. Now rest consciousness in the glowing chakra of white light above the head, Sarasrara Chakra, Kether, the Tenth Sephira of the Dayside Tree, seen as a glowing globe of astral energy and light.

Dancing with Genies, the Zar, the Loa and Demons of Abramelin

Throughout the course of history there are many that have seduced and been seduced by lovers from the spirit world–whether angels or demons, who can know? Manual magick is the formula for those who wish to dance with demons and with Jinn, to seduce the Loa and the serpent Nagas of the earth, and to create for themselves familiars to carry forward their desires. Needless to say, this is a perilous path...

The thread of human history is shot through with tales of contact with transmundane entities, angels, spirits, demons, ghosts, goddesses and gods, E.T.'s and fairy folk of heavenly, i.e. extraterrestrial origin, come down to mortal humans from the stars. Numerous accounts exist: *The Bible, The Necronomicon, A True & Faithful Relation* by Dee & Kelly, *The Sacred Magick of Abra-Melin the Mage,* and *Liber AL.*

"In Tibetan Buddhist Darkest Tantra, as you know, there is also a dancing with demons, with the Chod Dakinis and Cittapattis and Nagas

who either kill you or you transform oneself into a multidimensional being who can never truly die. Only the ego dies," explains GLH in a private communication. The Jinn, sometimes also called Genies are those geniuses or spirits that King Solomon bound and described in his Lesser Key. Their sigils, potencies and powers and suggested methods of working with them as well as expected results are detailed in the Shadow Tarot's Minor Arcana, in which they play the principle part.

Roots of Star Magick lie in West Africa. The West African and Caribbean Spirit Cults of Yemaya, Oshun and Erzulie grew out of the ancient Mysteries of Isis. Isis was believed by the Priests of the Old Ones to exist in a wet and swampy parallel universe and appeared to her devotees as an alluring reptilian water witch. The ancient devotees of Isis were sorcerers who mated with extraterrestrials, giving birth to the race of heroes, demi-gods and daemons alluded to in the *Egyptian Book of the Dead.* Kenneth Grant, in *Aleister Crowley and the Hidden God* states that the Isiac Currents are gathering strength about the astral atmosphere of the earth and that members of her cult are readying to propagate a new race of beings able to probe extra-terrestrial dimensions.

The Sirius Mystery explores the mythology of the Dogon tribe of Mali with its legends of contact with extraterrestrial beings from the binary star-system, Sirius, the Dog Star, Star of the Dark God Set. Sirius also figures importantly in the magickal writings of Kenneth Grant, and in Aleister Crowley's own traffic with transmundane intelligences: Amalantarah, Aiwass, Abul-Diz, LAM. In *Hecate's Fountain,* Kenneth Grant speaks of the planet Emme Ya in the Sirius star-system as the origin of the Loa, Voudoo goddesses and gods, the Orisha in Yoruba tradition who are "presently concerned with infiltrating the aura of earth." *Emme Ya* is the planet from which came the primal goddess, *Yemaya.* Her name, "Mother of Fish" recalls the ancient amphibious Nommos, powerful beings of god-like stature who

brought civilization to earth from the star system of Sirius and whom the Babylonians knew as the *Musari*.

Voudoo is a religion of possession. Its practitioners open the gates to Stellar Contacts, the Loa, and invite their goddesses and gods to mount and possess them, to come down upon their heads and ride. Thus they commune intimately with their gods, the Loa, contacting directly in the numinous present the ancient stream of consciousness that first penetrated this planet from Outside.

Zar spirits were known many thousands of years ago in Ancient Egypt where incense was burned, drums and cymbals played to exorcise these spirits from the humans they possessed. The Zar spirits and the Loa have many points in common and are in many ways unique. They each have their origins in African mysticism and religion, veiled from us by mists of time. They are not to be invoked. Instead, the Zar spirits and the Loa themselves choose the physical vehicle they would have. I emphasize that one does not choose but is chosen by the spirits themselves. You may read and study, do the rituals, prepare the altars and the offerings and you will benefit from doing all these things. However, that does not change the simple fact that you must be called by the spirits themselves. The relationship may be a one-off experience, or it may last a lifetime. Instead of possession, the spirits "mount" upon the devotee and then they "ride." Once mounted, the devotee becomes the physical vehicle for the spirits, much as Zora Neale Hurston has described in *Tell My Horse*, and as have many others recounted in similar tales of spirit possession by the Loa and the Zar.

Depending upon the nature of the Loa or Zar spirit, the spirit may desire to have the experience of sex using the body of the devotee as their physical vehicle. If this appears strange to onlookers to see and interact with someone so ridden or possessed, this relationship seems even more strange from the inside looking out. For the one possessed retains complete self-awareness while totally surrendered to the

passion, needs and desires of the possessing spirit as demanded by the nature of the spirit. This is experienced as a sort of dual consciousness, consisting of the both possessing spirit and the one possessed. Once so chosen by the spirits, the relationship is lifelong and will intersect the life of the devotee in many ways not limited to ritual. The freedom and exhilarating passion, the wondrous sense of soaring above the mundane world that one experiences when mounted by the spirits comes with an admittedly small price. The devotee must continue to honor the Loa and Zar spirits by allowing the possessing spirits to ride and possess the body, surrendering body, soul and Will with utter and complete abandon.

And so we find that there is power in seeking contact with those transmundane Intelligences that mutely dwell in the vastness of dark space between the stars. The use of vevers, magickal designs and linear patterns to identify, honor and call upon the spirits, demons, angels and gods springs from ancient memory patterns implanted in cells and blood and bones. These sigils were developed and in use long ago for establishing earth-contact with sentient stellar streaming, with those great transmundane intelligences who in their time-traveling first seeded terra with DNA. These great interdimensional beings are the Ancient Ones, the Outer Contacts, "the Gods of the Shadow." Timetables of extraterrestrial contact have rapidly compressed as human population has exploded. Human consciousness has multiplied, accelerating at a rate which will soon turn on the planetary exo-system and activate the consciousness of sleeping, dreaming Gaia, as we draw daily closer to the Comity of Stars.

The Practice: From within the protection of your circle, focus your intention on the chosen sigil as you work your manual magick, forging the connection at the moment of orgasm to propel you through the sigil's open gate into the vever's interdimensional alternate world. To return to mundane reality, make the Sign of Silence to enclose yourself

in a bright blue soap-like bubble of astral light. Tightly shut your eyes and then blink them open suddenly. Be not frightened by the visions you may then receive nor the sounds to which you may be subjected. Record your visions.

SEDUCING THE DEMON LOVER

The Demon Lover is seduced by invoking your Holy Guardian Angel (HGA) into the body of your lover via the sexual act, as your lover becomes a vessel for the HGA to fill. The Holy Guardian Angel is mysterious and deep, whole, transcendent, and truly "other," best approached by waiting, in silence and in "absence." Many think of the HGA as belonging to dayside ego-consciousness. One must have an integrated personality before one can safely pursue the magickal path, this is true, but this is only a starting-point to communion with the HGA. The HGA however is not of the dayside personality or personal ego. The HGA is not of the "little self," but of the *transpersonal ego*. It is that part of us which reincarnates from existence to existence, the immortal, eternal Self that lay behind the ever-changing personal masks and is our link to that first sentient stellar stream of consciousness that seeded our race and ever seeks to draw us outward to Itself.

In seeding human consciousness with the ability to link with stellar consciousness came the ability to form a direct link with the experience of the Holy Guardian Angel. "Who" or "what" is it that we connect with? It comes as a feeling of "otherness," of alienness. It is not that one has come in touch with one's innermost self, but that one has touched an emptiness, an acceptance, a vastness, an omniscience, a "knowing," with a sigh of release, one has "come home." The individual "belongs" to the HGA and not the other way around. Their vastness may encompass many human souls despite our feeling of individuality and uniqueness, imparting a feeling of rightness and destiny in the fabric of our lives, however fortunate or unfortunate that destiny may

prove to be in relation to the mundane world.

The HGA "incarnates" into your lover via mystic channeling as your lover manifests the HGA into flesh and blazes with etheric fire at the moment of orgasm. Gazing steadily into your lover's eyes project energy and intention through your right eye and pull that energy back to you through the left as you weave an ensnaring web of light emanating from your womb to fill the Universe. Regarding whether the sexual partner should be an Initiate, A.C. in *Magick Without Tears* notes, "that it is better and easier that the other party should be in ignorance of the sacred character of the Office." One may agree or not. Approach each experience with an open mind and record your results.

The Secret of Sekhmet and Immortality

Once the physical connection with the HGA has successfully been completed via orgasm with your chosen lover, the rite may be continued on the astral using the connection that has been previously created and your HGA is precipitated onto the astral. Invoke the mask of the Goddess Sekhmet as your HGA is materialized into the flesh of your lover and learn the secret of the Goddess Sekhmet and Immortality.

Sekhmet, the most ancient of gods was the first vampire. Sekhmet walked among men and drank their blood. Night after night Sekhmet waded in blood, slaughtering humans, drinking their blood. They could find no way to stop Sekhmet who was drunk on human blood. Sekhmet, Goddess Who Grants Desires, is the most ancient of goddesses and gods, older by far than Isis, Kali, Durga, Kwan Yin.

The invocation of Sekhmet, Goddess of the South, Flame of the Dark God Set, Lord of the Abyss and the Night of Time serves as the gateway to alien realms. Call upon the Goddess Sekhmet to raise Kundalini via ecstasy of the body to unite with cosmic consciousness. Sekhmet, Babalon the Great, Lady of the Scarlet-colored Garment, Goddess of sexual passion and strong drink, Mistress of the Gods,

Uncreated, Mightier than Gods.

To seek immortality in the living flesh, channel the Goddess Sekhmet in your sexual rites. Place an image of Lion-headed Sekhmet upon your altar. Light a red candle in her name. Make offerings of Red wine, Red beer, Red meat, Spicy and exotic foods, Pomegranates and Pomegranate juice, Ginger and Cinnamon. Call upon her by her names: Eye of Ra, The Red Lady, She At Whose Wish the Arts were Born, Lady of Enchantments, Destroyer by Plagues, Powerful One Before Whom Evil Trembles, Mistress of Dread, Lady of Slaughter. Wear her sacred colors red, and gold and her sacred stones: Fire Agate, Bloodstone, Carnelian, Fluorite, Garnet, Hematite, Red Jasper, Ruby, Tiger's Eye. Wear her perfumes: Amber, Cardamom, Frankincense, Lotus, Myrrh, Patchouli, Sandalwood. Ply your cat with catnip!

Burn to her Kyphi Incense (Kyphi Tsa–From Ancient Egyptian Traditional List)

Ingredients: 6 oz Honey, 3 Raisins, 2 oz Copal, 2 oz Myrrh, 2 oz tsp Orris Root,

8 oz Sandalwood, 2 oz Storax, 4 oz Frankincense, 4 oz Cinnamon.

Thoroughly grind and mix together all ingredients. Add enough red wine to moisten.

Roll into 5/8" balls. Roll balls in benzoin. Lay out on waxed paper for a week or so, until firm.

To burn, set on lighted charcoal.

CAUTION: Incense balls will look like yummy donut holes. NOT edible!

Qulielfi
From *The Shadow Tarot* by Linda Falorio

Characith
From *The Shadow Tarot* by Linda Falorio

Blood Magick, Moon Magick

Meditate on the Tunnel of Characith[1], domain of boundless energy and creativity, personal magnetism and eternal youth, ruled by the inconstant Moon, the light in darkness with the ultimate power of feminine attraction, as bearer and transmitter of the Blood. The feminine powers of generation and regeneration mirror the Moon in its monthly phases. The release of the ovum is the Full Moon, symbolic of fertility, while menstruation is of the Dark of the Moon, a time of blighting and of death. The baleful "Moon-dew" used by Thessalian witches in their curses was comprised of a girl's first menstrual blood taken during the eclipse of the Moon. The menstruating woman has been universally feared from ancient times unto the present. The frightful onset of bleeding when there was no wound was experienced with fear and awe, and believed to possess powerful magic. Psychic insights manifest as extreme emotional states that are common at this time. Some Native American cultures, however, recognized this as a time of great power, and accorded much importance to the dreams that women had during their bleeding times, this mysterious energy that might prove to be beneficent, or, could turn maleficent, had to somehow be kept within bounds.

Characith conceals the mystery of the deep identity of male and female as complimentary energy systems. In the mystery of the identity of phallus with kteis, and of the corpora cavernosa/clitoris in the female with the prostatic glands/prostate in the male, lies the secret of distilling the elixir of ecstasy and magickal immortality. The elixir may be used has been used to create vampires of those who linger here to drink. The elixir reminds us of practices associated with blood, with the eclipsed moon and menstruation, and the physical result of

---

[1] Characith corresponds to the tarot card, The Chariot, on the "Nightside of the Tree of Life" as elaborated by Kenneth Grant in his book *Nightside of Eden*.

the long confinement to the night, for they too easily become addicted to the pleasures of pursuance of their dark desires. The day before menstruation, the gates between the worlds are thrown open and the magician is most vulnerable to vampirism of every kind. Draining life to sustain energy and life beyond its ordinary span, these acquire the power of bewitchment, casting strong enchantments to lure fresh victims to their astral touch. For the vampire's secret of eternal life lies in the power to appropriate the energy of others—their very lifeblood through sexual contact. Beware of astral sex with demons, for the danger is physical exhaustion at their touch, of becoming drained at the tongues of vampires more adept at appropriating energies than oneself, of obsession and possession, of having your life taken over in ways unimagined and unimaginable. You have been officially warned. Yet the temptation is great, for in touching the deep feminine on the astral plane where they most easily manifest, all one's desires are instantly met in a world of one's own creation.

Please note: there are many ways to distill the requisite elixirs and many uses for each vintage as they cycle through the monthly moon. I personally have found the use of the astral elixirs distilled through these sexual rites to be much preferred over the purely physical, though some may find it more convenient to use physical manifestation as their point of focus to access astral realities.

Tree of Night Tantra via Eroto-Comatose Orgasmica

Now in communion with the Angel of your Higher Self, bring yourself to orgasm in each of the nine centers, without anxiety, without guilt, either alone or with the assistance of your lover. Record your visions. Take your time, as you may want to experience each orgasm several times, as you gather in the powers that each bestows. Don't combine the practices into one orgasmic experience, as it requires nine distinct

orgasms to achieve the full effect. To intensify the experience, explore the practice of eroto-comatose lucidity, where orgasm is delayed for as long as possible in order to obtain profound psychic awareness and paranormal abilities, such as astral projection, precognition, thought transference, while in the twilight trance state that is thus induced.

To orgasm through the chakras rather than through the sexual organs, the most common focus of sensation requires quite a bit of training and control. However, if you have practiced the preceding exercises you should be easily able to direct your magickal intention.

1. Orgasm through the base of the spine. This etheric energy center corresponds to Malkuth and the Muladhara chakra. To orgasm through this center gives the power of tantric energy exchange. Here is the power of distilling the transforming elixir as the semiochemicals of the sexual kalas pour forth from your body and the Silver Rain of Nuit falls down upon you from the stars.

2. Orgasm through the center below the navel. This etheric energy center corresponds to The Knot of Brahma. To orgasm through this energy center gives personal power, the experience of Ch'i as tentacles of light radiating from your Center, reaching out to objects of your attention and desire. To orgasm here brings the power to "see" yourself and other humans as glowing luminous eggs of light, interconnected nodes, vortices of sentience, throbbing with the rhythm of life.

3. Orgasm through the navel. This etheric energy center corresponds to Yesod, the Ninth Sephira upon the Dayside Tree and Svadisthana Chakra. To orgasm through this energy center gives powers of fascination and enchantment, of imagination kindled by desire, the power to create illusions, to create one's own universe–be it heaven, or, be it hell. In this center is power to experience the "juiciness" of life,

its richness, and the sensuousness inherent in all that flows: emotions, rivers, blood.

4. Orgasm through the diaphragm. This etheric energy center corresponds to the Veil of Paroketh, the Knot of Vishnu and Manipura Chakra. To orgasm through this energy center gives the power of speech in silence, the power of invisibility, the power of the shroud. To orgasm here gives power to enter outré dimensions via the cosmological Black Hole of interstellar space, of matter collapsed upon itself by the power of internal attraction.

5. Orgasm through the compassionate heart. This etheric energy center corresponds to Tiphareth, the Sixth Sephira on the Dayside Tree, The Crossroads and Anahata Chakra. To orgasm here gives the power of invisibility, the power of entering another's body, heart and mind, and the power to experience the reality of Self as nothing more than an Ego-less Void.

6. Orgasm through the throat area. This etheric energy center corresponds to the Knot of Shiva, Vishudda Chakra and Daäth, the entrance to "Universe B" and the Tunnels of Set. To orgasm through this energy center gives the power of the shaman, the power of shape-shifting, the power of cosmic transmutation of the primal cell. To orgasm here is the power to touch and experience the combined female-male as nascent possibility within one's own body of light. To send one's consciousness here is knowledge of past-present-future as existent in the Now.

7. Orgasm through the third eye. This etheric energy center corresponds to Twin-petalled Binah/Chokmah and Ajna Chakra situated at the center of the brow. To orgasm here gives power to

enter the Dream Time; and to leave the body at will; to externalize, objectify and universalize one's internal, subjective and highly personal conception of reality. Orgasm here brings power to utter the "birth words" of Master of the Temple.

8. Orgasm through the crown of the head. This etheric energy center corresponds to Kether and Thousand-petalled Sarasrara Chakra. To orgasm here, raise Kundalini up the spine, allowing consciousness to pour out through the top of the skull into the exploding universe, the ever-expanding shower of stars. To orgasm through this energy center is to experience the light and energy of the Stars above as source of inspiration and spiritual sustenance, the seeding of our race. Orgasm here brings the power of trans-dimensional, interstellar time-travel.

9. Orgasm through every pore of your body, experiencing the interconnecting points of singing light that cover the living flesh. To orgasm here is to feel the vibrating *nadis* of the subtle body, tiny pricklings of light that are the blessings of the kalas of the stars as they rain down from transplutonian dimensions. Feel the fireworks as they impinge upon your body; see in them the image of the universe alive with whirling, pulsing many-colored stars. Orgasm here brings the power of calling the *Great Old Ones,* timeless travelers, the gods who are ever returning, spiraling from past and future into an eternally unfolding now.

Twilight Magick

In Twilight dimensions of awareness accessed in trance and magickal sleep, we may open a deep and long-forgotten gateway via *Daäth* to call upon the Outer Contacts. Channeling through the magician's lens of awakened consciousness and Will, we invite these vast transcendent beings to once more intersect our world. Through such a series of

magickal workings by the Pittsburgh Group, directed toward contact with LAM and the Maatian Current an ancient sigil was received, a form of the Voudoo vever of the Marassa, the Twins of the Aeon of Zain, its ritual use dating from Atlantis. The magickal activation of this sigil through the rites described activated a long disused Stellar Gateway deep in the Shenandoah Mountains through which the primal Goddess of Space emerged, awakened into our dimension.

Cross the Abyss from Tiphareth to Kether via Daäth at the dark time of the Moon when the Stellar Current most potently penetrates our conscious field *via* the 13th path of the Priestess, Gimel, Neptune, Moon, path of "Khonsu, the Strider of the Stars," the Traveler of the Night Sky. Call upon Legba, God of the Crossroads Carfax, the Point of Intersection, to open the Gate at the Point of Crossing, Tiphareth. And as Legba Ellegua Baron Samedi opens the Gate via Tiphareth, call upon Oxossi, intermediary between Inner and Outer stellar contacts, between what we know ourselves to be and adumbrations of far-future selves, time-travelers from a non-existent present to the distant stars, to open the Gate to Outside via Daäth that the Old Ones may pass from their universe into ours, and enter our consciousness dimension.

"Honi Soit Qui Mal y Pense."

You go, girls! And "Let Evil come to him who Evil thinks!"

Hemethterith
From *The Shadow Tarot* by Linda Falorio

![Strange Birth illustration]

Strange Birth by Emma Doeve

A Darker Magic

by Emma Doeve

"I didn't have time to be anyone's muse... I was too busy rebelling against my family and learning to be an artist."
— Leonora Carrington, 1983

Leonora Carrington (6th April 1917 - 25th May 2011) was an English painter, sculptor, and writer, and one of the more colourful personalities among the Women Surrealists. The product of a privileged background, and yet a natural eccentric from childhood, she rebelled against the debutante path set out for her to go to Paris and study Art. She met Picasso and Dali, falling in with the Surrealists–who recognised her precocious talent and tried to claim her as an avatar of their *femme enfant* and *sorciere*–and soon eloped with Max Ernst, despite his being 26 years her senior and already married.

With the outbreak of World War II, she became separated from Ernst during an attempt to escape Nazi Occupation–the shock and stress of which caused a mental breakdown, leading to incarceration in a Spanish psychiatric hospital, complete with barbaric drug treatment, shock therapy, and possible abuse.

After "being rescued by her nanny who arrived in a submarine," like many of the other Surrealists she relocated to Mexico, which became her primary home and inspiration for the remainder of her long life.

Always interested in the occult, her esoteric studies became ever-more central to her life and work–particularly in collaboration with her close friend, fellow painter Remedios Varo. Together they would explore the folk magic and markets of their adopted homeland, blending it with their readings in Alchemy, Cabala, and Gnosticism.

As well as being a painter, Leonora Carrington was a prolific writer, her deceptively fairytale-like or absurdist stories containing a distillation of her engagement with the worlds of myth, magic and dream. Her rendition of some of the events in her life "should not be understood literally, but as magic realism–a response to her own mental state and events at the time. There is a sense of a hybrid world half recognizable, half fantasy..."

It could be a definition of Surrealism itself.

The following is an extract from a longer piece of writing, 'My Evenings with Leonora'...

When Max Ernst, Leonora Carrington's lover, was taken away to a concentration camp for the second time during WWII, her life went into a tailspin. After a spell of purging and what we would now call detoxing, she left Nazi-occupied France to go to Madrid, to try and obtain a visa. Also, as she writes in *Down Below*,[1] Spain represented "Discovery" for her. Her companion at the time, an old friend, an English woman called Catherine, suggested that she harboured an unconscious desire to "eliminate the father" (in the person of Ernst, who was 26 years her senior).

"Eliminating the father" could be interpreted in terms of challenging patriarchy: masculine institutions and outmoded sexual assumptions.

Carrington herself is quoted as saying:

"The Bible, like any other history ... is full of gaps and peculiarities

---

1 Leonora Carrington, *Down Below* (February, 1944).

that only begin to make sense if understood as a covering-up for a very different kind of civilisation which has been eliminated."[2]

As events unfolded, it would seem as if life itself created the very circumstances by which Leonora Carrington had to undergo the painful but necessary process of Death and Loss, then Transformation and Danger, to experience in her *own* life, her *own* body, the evolution of female emancipation, before emerging stronger at the other end: before being Reborn, able to truly fulfil her creative potential.

> *The room is dark, with one candle burning on a low table. Sounds of gongs and singing bowls are drifting softly through the space.*
>
> *Deep down below, there is a great stirring. Initially I do not know what might emerge from the depths and in the anticipation there is fear and awe also, which is echoed by the profound soundscape of rising and falling waves, swelling and subsiding all around us.*
>
> *Gradually I sense the possibility that–to some extent–it is my choice what will be conjured up and arise to the surface. My imagination doesn't have to be completely passive.*

On the road to Spain, Carrington smells Death. She's travelling through a war-torn land and like it says in the song "people are strange when you're a stranger." They carry guns; they transport dead people. There is danger all around. She feels dissociated from her own body; mind and body seem to be breaking apart, and the strangers around her seem invested with an inexplicable power. She feels "jammed in the motions of her body" and begins to suffer vertigo when she and her companions reach mountainous country. She wants to overcome her vertigo, her sense of being paralysed, and sets about analysing what afflicts her, but finds that "her will is no longer geared with her faculties

---

[2] Whitney Chadwick, *Pilgrimage to the Stars: Leonora Carrington and the Occult Tradition* (1991).

of motion." But she must tackle and cross the mountain. Pure will, she realizes, won't do the trick. Something more organic is required. One morning she goes to the mountain alone, and after at first being hardly able to walk, she finds herself becoming stronger: she finds herself endowed with almost superhuman strength and energy, climbing the steep mountainside, jumping from rock to rock like a young Pan, being able to run and jump, "like a goat." She finds she can commune with, and draw near to, the animals, where other people can't. When they approach, the animals scamper away.

> That night, from waves of colour and a heavy earth I invoke and then slowly observe the head of a Minotaur emerging from below. Where I can see the top of its head, with the two great horns, the area is brightly lit, darkening as we move outwards.
>
> There is an air of suspense–everything is happening very slowly–almost to the measure of the subtle sound waves around us.
>
> The eyes of the Minotaur are still closed from its deep sleep, but I know that they are going to open. There is a terrible fear and excitement, apprehension, all at the same time.
>
> My fellow traveller finds himself in a rocky desert landscape, with a eunuch companion. The area is peopled by spindly, waif-like beings, hunted by powerfully-built four-armed creatures who, when they capture their quarry, pin them to the ground. The hunting and the fighting has an almost balletic grace. One of these creatures watches my companion, jumps forward towards him, and shows its vampire-like fangs.

In *Down Below*, Carrington finds herself among a growing number of refugees. She hallucinates: Spain is her kingdom, Madrid the city she must save; it is the world's stomach, and she must restore this organ back to health. She is its doctor, its saviour. What is particularly marked in her account is the combination of–and sometimes violent

oscillation between—on the one hand fear, torment, and general low self-esteem, and on the other megalomania and euphoria one moment, and unbearable anguish the next. She barely speaks the language, but as she says, "this makes it possible for her to invest the most ordinary phrases with hermetic significance." Her hallucinatory state, in which she dreams or imagines events and experiences that may or may not have happened, mimics the first stages of Initiation: loss, and disorientation, a dying to the old self.

> *He sees serpents, large, bejewelled and enamelled, coiling and curling upwards, around the naked bodies of dancing women.*
>
> *Silver rain is falling, downwards, then upwards, descending and ascending, in time with the deep breathing and the circular rhythm. The moisture forms an egg-like cocoon round his body, as the singing bowls and gongs generate their sound and light enters the chakras, opening and bringing them to life.*
>
> *Dark-blue crystalline pyramids swing into view, and we study the light refracting through them ...*

Leonora's Initiation continued as she travelled deeper into the Labyrinth. Legendary craftsman and artist Daedalus purpose-built its structure to hold the Minotaur, part-man, part-bull. Her adventures there would be truly harrowing, her spirit-guide testing her and her endurance to the limit. In one sense, she went truly mad, fighting real life and imaginary monsters tooth and nail, but she never lost herself. One reason was that her esoteric studies, beginning with alchemy when she was just a student, were real to her, providing a kind of map.[1]

> *The library, on its beetling height, is dedicated to scholars who have withdrawn from the world to copy and study rare manuscripts.*

---

[1] Special mention should be made of the sadly overlooked Surrealist writer, Pierre Mabille (1904-1952). Author of the classic Surrealist work on Myth, *Mirror of the Marvellous* (1940), he was a close friend who initiated Carrington into the Cabala.

The tower, going up and up and up . . . the more rare books are held in chambers higher up, and are harder to get to–a strange, winding, vertical labyrinth.

The ruins of an Abbey like Glastonbury, overrun by surprisingly lush, decidedly tropical vegetation. I am pursuing the mysterious figure of a woman–tall, dark, enigmatic, ever-receding–leading me slowly yet steadily and inexorably in to the darker, hidden recesses. . .There is some cognitive dissonance about her movements–and, by extension, mine in following her–which have that almost clichéd dream-like slow motion–and the growth and movement of the vegetation, which is like speeded-up, stop-motion photography, conveying the unrelenting proliferation of Nature in all Her irresistible, unstoppable, lush fecundity: the abandoned constructions of Man are drowning in the oncoming tide of vegetable life . . . It is like two layers or speeds of Time are superimposed, shown at once. When the sequence runs its course, The Woman has lead me to a dark, enclosed chamber at the centre of the ruins–like the Heart of the Labyrinth–where she squats, tending a sacred fire-pit. She is a tall, strong, powerfully built woman, attractive, with an almost primitive "noble savage" regal bearing about her–even as she hunkers down in her black cloak and tattered shawls, like an old crone, crooning over her cooking-pot or cauldron.

At the Heart of the Labyrinth by Emma Doeve

Mistress of Eros by Emma Doeve

The Dæmon Lover

by Emma Doeve

She went outside and into the Woods which started at the end of the garden, and then stood still and silent, breathing deeply for long minutes, then holding her breath till she could hold it no more. The Night was charged as never before, but she knew the charge lay primarily inside her.

She could smell the trees and the soil beneath her. It had rained earlier and even though it was night, it was still warm; some of the intense heat of the Sun had been trapped down below, and the Earth was moist and steaming, releasing a thousand elemental odours.

While she stood there, in the knuckle-white moonlight, the air balmy and fresh around her, it was as if she could feel Him slip out of her body and start to move among the trees. She could feel and sense His presence, like a shape of shadow, yet more substantial than a shadow. He might appear in actuality at any second. The anticipation was almost unbearable. The vibrations that passed through her, discharging themselves from time to time like electrical currents, were mounting and becoming almost insupportable. She shivered, but it wasn't from being cold.

What would it be like to actually see Him? And why did it fill her with apprehension? Had she not been aware of Him for the longest time? She knew He could–and would–transform himself into many shapes, both light and dark, a presence half-human, half-animal, or half-god, half-demon...

It started early, when I was still a child. I would sit together with a bunch of other girls and they would talk about their dolls, and how they would have children, and be mums and nurses, as soon as they grew up. When they would ask me, and I told them I neither owned nor wanted any dolls, and that having babies was definitely *not* on my mind, they would look at me with an unmistakable distaste, mounting to revulsion, on their faces. Soon I would be branded, and often made to feel like, an outsider among my own sex.

We moved to a new home, situated in an urban wasteland which had claimed and despoiled what had once been a real wilderness, not far from the sea. After school, I would go out to where there was still some rough ground left, and start digging. I didn't quite know *what* I was looking for, except that it was Ancient, and had once been alive, and *strong*. Maybe–whatever it was I was searching for–had once been my friend and protector, and had been lost down there. Once, I invited a girlfriend to come and play in the sands with me, to have, as I suggested to her, an adventure. I lit a small fire with what dry grass and sticks I could find, and then started to dig, saying we might, perhaps, find some treasure. What we found–or, rather, what *I* found–were bones, small ones, probably from a rabbit. The girl who had been standing by, idly, now looked over her shoulder, nervously. When she saw the pale, earth-stained bones, she freaked out, and ran and told everybody what a creep she thought I was. All that mattered to me, however, was that I was disappointed at my find. I wanted to find *bigger* bones, giant-sized bones, befitting the dreams I was having. In one of them I had discovered a colossal skull, fantastically hung with exotic jewels. It could have been a dragon's head. I crept behind the empty eye-sockets, and looked through them, and saw a fantastic world.

Not for the first time, I sought refuge in art and books and music. Woods or hills or wild water all being harder to come by where I grew up. And grown-up Magic was still an undiscovered territory on the

map, largely, though I had heard distant rumours. In my family, Magic had once been intertwined with daily life, even death: but that had been another world, in a tropical land halfway across the globe, a world they had to leave behind...

There were others like me, but I didn't even know. There were people long dead—artists, mystics, poets—who were more real to me than the people I was with, dangerously so. Later, much later, I would find *some* like myself alive in the present, or at least I would become aware of them.

All through my young years I would hear: an artist has his Muse, a woman may be a Muse to an artist, but as Robert Graves wrote, taking it one step further still:

"Woman is not a poet; she is either a Muse or she is nothing."

She may even be an artist herself. But who or what is her inspiration? And what shape would it take?

Although the Surrealist artist Leonora Carrington said she was too busy learning to be an artist to be anyone's muse, when asked how she felt about the "official" Surrealist identification of Woman and Muse, her succinct reply was "bullshit." Likewise, fellow artist and occult explorer Ithell Colquhoun remarked that the:

"...vision of the 'free and adored woman' didn't always prove a practical help for women, especially painters."

The question remained: *who* or *what* inspired the female artist that would be on a par with the male artist's Muse? Not that the female artists seemed to lack 'inspiration.' It became clear that centuries of having been the subject of male fantasy, and the male artist's muse, model, or groupie, had taken their toll. What women artists wanted and were mostly portraying—that is, if they portrayed the human form at all—was themselves. They wanted a sweet revenge of a kind—or often *not* so sweet—to tell their own stories, and set the record straight. It seemed they couldn't get enough of it.

From the moment I first heard it, I was intrigued: beneath an eerie moon, the poet Coleridge wrote in *Kubla Khan* of a "woman wailing for her demon-lover!" She is maddened by lust, desire, beside herself–or else why would she be *wailing* for that demon lover?–But it is still a *man's* vision: Coleridge the poet has been feminized, and luxuriates in the sacred, secret access of female emotion.

The setting is a primeval chasm, an enchanted site of black magic, lit by a waning moon. It's a dangerous point of contact, where the human and non-human meet. A connection between biology and geology has been made: our sex-impulses spring from the same elemental forces that shape the very Earth.

I pictured the scene: the cleft in the Earth, the Moon behind scudding clouds, releasing her magical beams from time to time–interrupted by the branches of a few twisted trees–the light never *quite* reaching the bottom of the chasm, where the woman crouched until she saw and heard the "demon lover" approach, above her on the rim of the dell.

One night, during my time of the month, I made my way to a lonely place in the hills and found a hollow in the earth under some juniper trees. The silvery Moon hanging high in the West was half full, and the sky was studded with what seemed like thousands of stars. Obeying a call of nature, I hunkered down and mingled my body's fluids with the earth below. I looked up, and from the unfathomable stars came distant echoes, filling the air with invisible genies, while blood and water ran down the rocks, before sinking into the ground. I felt I was making an offering, seeking a union, but to what, to whom?

The incubus, we know, is a male demon who visits women at night, and lies upon sleepers in order to have sexual intercourse with them. They could be sylvan, faun, elemental, or other demonic entity; sometimes they may even take the shape of your loved one. This male demon also transforms himself into a female entity, it is said, to visit men at night, while they're sleeping, and steal their semen. Sexual

relations are the norm, but in the story the woman is always passive and unconscious.

Would it be possible to become less passive to this demonic influence, to dare to wake up, and stay awake and somehow record the encounter, even if it happened entirely in the imagination? Even take charge, be the active agent? The night visitor prefers or even needs our unconscious, because the unconscious is where He lives. The unconscious is where He has his roots.

How dangerous would it be to try and stay conscious and aware, and face Him? Too scary, too dangerous, apparently. It is likely that most women feel there is *enough* male danger in the real world already, to want to deal with a dark, dangerous stranger within their own selves.

At this point, a matter of semantics needs to be settled, if it can be settled at all. It concerns the very word that might define a female artist's creative spirit, a candidate that might qualify as a counterpart to the Muse:

The word "Daimôn" or "Dæmon" is a Latinized version of a Greek word from Classical mythology, where it has a benevolent or benign connotation, originally, generally related to ghosts, chthonic heroes, or spirit guides: great and powerful figures might become "Daimôn" after their death.

But according to *Greek Religion* by Harvard scholar Walter Burkert, apparently a 5th century "doctor" offered the priceless insight that:

"neurotic women and girls can be driven to suicide by imaginary apparitions, 'evil daimones.'"

Here the other, more familiar, concept of the Christian "Demon"–with its dark, negative associations and implications–has swung into view.

There are a few reports of and testimonies by women who've attempted a full-on encounter with their creative dæmon or daimôn. The brilliant scholar Camille Paglia wrote a piece about Sylvia Plath's

poem, *Daddy*, in which she says that:

"*...the energies aroused by 'Daddy' ultimately become self-devouring. The poem is so extreme that nothing can be built upon it.*"

In the end the demonic *Daddy*-even with "a stake in your fat black heart"-survives, and the poet loses her dispute for mental territory. Unlike what the Feminist camp, which might want to claim her as entirely their own, likes to believe, Plath had great respect for some of the best male writers-and yet still she committed suicide in the house where her beloved Yeats had once lived.

In her breakthrough opus, *Sexual Personae,* Paglia writes concerning *Wuthering Heights,* that there's an impasse about this novel among the critics, "with many moral and sexual issues unresolved." There is also disagreement about nearly *everything* in the book, because there has been a reluctance to ask biographical questions about its author, Emily Brönte. Paglia makes an interesting, innovative suggestion: that in the novel, Brönte hermaphroditizes herself into her anti-hero, who is seen as a "ghoul or a vampire." Again, the suggestion is that such extremism may well have been career and possibly life-ending. Brönte refused to live in the pleasant ordered Victorian present. She died the year after the book was published.

The case of how to find the creative Daimôn to counterbalance the Muse (in fact there are *nine* of them) remains a Sleeping Giant. Attention is turned elsewhere.

The territory of the Daimôn remains mostly unexplored, the Daimôn himself unrealized, untamed.

The dreams of dragons and serpents continue, and they may become vaguely threatening-which points to a very particular peril: that our freshly acquired consciousness is in danger of being swallowed up *again* by the instinctual soul and our primitive selves...

Eventually and inevitably I became aware of Tantra, with its ancient and sophisticated knowledge of the erotic arts, where initiation-

invariably by engagement with the feminine–is considered a form of spiritual instruction.

Indian spirituality did not labour under the Judeo-Christian attitude, which demonized the flesh and viewed the body, if not with fear, disgust or horror, then certainly with a kind of contempt. The fusion between the sexual and the sacred has always been problematic in the West–with a few notable exceptions, perhaps, like the *Song of Songs*, which is viewed usually as an allegory between God and His people, or God and the soul, conveniently bypassing the sexual desire and intimacy that is expressed in the text.

People have come to Tantra by different routes. What is certain is that a whole generation of Western men and women found their way to Yoga and Tantra through the more generous and sexually open climate created in the Sixties and thereafter, up to the present day.

In spite of what the so-called pious may think Jerusalem had never vanquished Babylon.

And after Tantra, comes Kundalini, the Fire Serpent.

"We come to Magick as sexual beings," writes Margaret Ingalls, aka Nema, going on to say that: "To delay using our sexual powers in our Magick until we've attained a particular Magickomystical milestone makes no sense to me."

I have not come to this territory, by which I mean the Sex-Magickal, by way of the permissive and explorative culture that emerged from the Sixties... Mine has been a more organic and solitary journey. For the first experience and encounter with the Fire Serpent, I have to reach back in time, to when I would not even have used the name, not being aware of it, as I am now.

There had been sustained and intense reading of a particular piece of writing, the strange poem *Epipsychidion* by Percy Shelley, as well as other esoteric, mystical, and even occult texts, and there had been inward reflection and meditation over many days. It was Christmas,

and I was cooped up in an apartment with other people, all of whom had time off, like myself. And through the thin walls I could hear and sense many others, all in some kind of holiday torpor. The atmosphere was vapid, spiritless, and flat.

I was alone in my room, and there were no distractions except the banal sounds of everyday, nothing to draw my attention away from what I was doing or going through. Nothing seemed to touch me from the outside, except now and then when I would hear a certain kind of music to which my senses–what senses I couldn't tell exactly–seemed unnaturally susceptible, to the point of pain, but it was a delectable pain. Inwardly, I was totally absorbed. A kind of energy was waking up in me, and I didn't know what was happening, except that some tremendous force was passing through me. It lasted for an hour or so, and then began to subside.

A few evenings later–New Year's Eve, in fact–I remember with great clarity: I was hiding in my room, dreading the moment someone would knock on my door and tell me it was time to leave, as we were meant to be going to visit some relatives to 'celebrate' the turning of the year. I could pretend I was ill, but it wouldn't have changed anything about the way I was feeling.

What I was experiencing was so intense, I was literally afraid I would die of it. I sat as quietly as I could while it assailed me–that is the only way I can describe it. Every two minutes or so, my blood turned into Fire, consuming and piercing and burning me within, with such sweetness and vehemence, it was unbearable. There was nothing I could have done, no protection against this Fire. I only wished and prayed for strength. I knew somehow that something, something rising from the depth of my bowels, was preparing me, though again, for what, I didn't know. I only knew that my body could not endure this living fire for much longer, without passing out or worse.

Would it have made a difference if someone had told me that it

might have been the Kundalini serpent, unwinding its three-and-a-half coils from the base of my spine, that it was the Shakti-energy sending its waves of bliss through my body? Probably not...

Being neither completely of East or West, I arrived at that place from a different direction, by a different route–perhaps one all my own–although I have since explored some of the vast territory of Tantra and Yoga, reserving a special place for the Fire Serpent, and there is, of course, the whole Tradition of Western Sex-Magick: of Crowley, and Evola, and Fortune, and Grosche, Parsons-Cameron, Randolph, Spare, and others...

Sampling the eccentric delights of Kenneth Grant's approach to these matters has become a favourite pastime!

Best of all is finding a lover with whom to share the Magick, and its pleasures and challenges.

Best of All is finding a way to the demon-lover, and taking on the dæmon, or daimôn, or even demon, and *not* succumbing–meeting on equal terms, and being able to Create from it.

I am committed to the continuing struggle and search...

– April 2014

Gestation by Sharmon Davidson-Jennings

Lucifer's Lover

by Diane Narraway

Son of the Morning

Those from Abrahamic backgrounds will undoubtedly have come across Lucifer, often synonymous with Satan or the Christian Devil who although he allegedly originated as the light bearer, the first, most beautiful angel who Yahweh loved above all the other angels fell from grace for his pride and arrogance. Lucifer then goes on to lead a rebellion in heaven thus creating the divide between angel and demon.

All archetypal imagery portrays Lucifer either before his fall from grace as a beautiful blonde shining angel or afterwards as a horned, sometimes winged demon usually with more animalistic features than human. The animal imagery is taken from Cernunnos the horned guardian of the wild forest, Pan the sexually driven satyr of Arcadia, the sacred Ibex of Arabia and later as the Sabbatic goat-Baphomet. The blonde angelic appearance has no such defined origins and is solely based on the concept of light and purity and of course all that is pure is beautiful. His fall is the first warning that through pride and arrogance something so Beautiful becomes beast.

The only biblical reference to his fall from grace is in the following passage from Isaiah 14:

12. How art thou fallen from heaven, O Lucifer, son of the morning! how art thou cut down to the ground, which didst weaken the nations!

13. For thou hast said in thine heart, I will ascend into heaven, I will exalt my throne above the stars of God: I will sit also upon the mount of the congregation, in the sides of the north:

14. I will ascend above the heights of the clouds; I will be like the most High.

15. Yet thou shalt be brought down to hell, to the sides of the pit.

16. They that see thee shall narrowly look upon thee, and consider thee, saying, Is this the man that made the earth to tremble, that did shake kingdoms;

17. That made the world as a wilderness, and destroyed the cities thereof; that opened not the house of his prisoners?

18. All the kings of the nations, even all of them, lie in glory, every one in his own house.

19. But thou art cast out of thy grave like an abominable branch, and as the raiment of those that are slain, thrust through with a sword, that go down to the stones of the pit; as a carcase trodden under feet.

20. Thou shalt not be joined with them in burial, because thou hast destroyed thy land, and slain thy people: the seed of evildoers shall never be renowned.

21. Prepare slaughter for his children for the iniquity of their fathers; that they do not rise, nor possess the land, nor fill the face of the world with cities.

Although it says Lucifer it is generally considered that it is more likely to be a reference to the Babylonian King Nebuchadnezzar, possibly Babylon itself but certainly not Lucifer. This is because in the original Hebrew text it is "the shining one, son of the dawn." While this may possibly translate as the morning star or indeed as Lucifer in the Latin Vulgate, when King James translated the bible instead of accurately translating from the Latin Lucifer to the English 'Morning Star' he retained the proper noun Lucifer.

At this point it is worth mentioning that the KJV was translated by nearly 50 different scholars following instructions that this translation was to reflect the current church of England doctrine...unfortunately this was translated during the burning times when the pact with the devil was a key factor in witch trials. It is also worth noting that this is the same bible that brought us Exodus 22:18:

'though shalt not suffer a witch to live' which in the Latin Vulgate actually reads 'thou shalt not suffer evil food'.

Rightly or wrongly this begins the link from Lucifer to Satan which then continues with Luke 10:18:

And he said to them, "I saw Satan fall like lightning from heaven.

19. Behold, I have given you authority to tread on serpents and scorpions, and over all the power of the enemy, and nothing shall hurt you.

20. Never the less, do not rejoice in this, that the spirits are subject to you, but rejoice that your names are written in heaven."

And as extra back up there is always Satan's desire to be God which can be found in Genesis 3:5:

For God doth know that in the day ye eat thereof, then your eyes shall be opened, and ye shall be as gods, knowing good and evil.

Having established the link albeit tenuous between Lucifer and Satan, the fact remains that nowhere in the bible is Lucifer's arrogance and alleged fall from grace as the first angel recorded, so why is it such a widely accepted story.

It appears to have its roots in other areas including an ancient Canaanite myth where the morning star is depicted as the god Attar, whose failed attempts to occupy the throne of Ba'al result in his descent as ruler of the underworld. Equally Ishtar or Inanna's descent into the underworld may have contributed plus they are both associated with the planet Venus. Although the most likely contender for the mythos surrounding Lucifer being cast out of heaven for his arrogance and pride comes from the Qu'ran creation myth which features what is possibly erroneously said to be a 'rebel angel' called Iblis, this also links him to his most famous alter ego...Satan.

The story teaches us that angels do not have free will and therefore cannot sin because they were not granted the freedom by God to disobey, so when God created Adam, he commanded all the angels and Iblis (who is Djinn but whose rank allowed him to be considered equal to that of an angel) to prostrate to Adam who was termed "the Best of Creation." All the angels did so but Iblis refused to obey, and was brought into a state of rebellion against God. For this defiance God cast him out of paradise with the intention of damning him to Hell for all eternity but Iblis begged God to delay the punishment until the Last Judgment, to which God agreed. Iblis then vowed that he would use this time to lead all men and women astray to Hell as a way of revenge against them. Upon his exile from paradise and he became known as "Shaytan."

(Allah) said: "What prevented thee from prostrating when I

commanded thee?" He said: "I am better than he: Thou didst create me from fire and him from clay."

He said: "Give me respite till the day they are raised up."

(Allah) said: "Be thou among those who have respite."

He said: "Because thou hast thrown me out of the way, lo! I will lie in wait for them on thy straight way:

"Then will I assault them from before them and behind them, from their right and their left: Nor wilt thou find, in most of them, gratitude (for thy mercies)."

(Allah) said: "Get out from this, disgraced and expelled. If any of them follow thee–Hell will I fill with you all."

Shaytan refers to an entity that is rebellious–irrespective of whether it is human, djinn, angel or animal. It is 'a nefarious soul' who through its actions becomes distanced from Allah and therefore distanced from 'Truth.' Shaytan is a 'common noun' whereas Iblis is a 'proper noun.' In other words, every harmful, deviating and rebellious entity–human or otherwise–is referred to as Shaytan. Iblis is the name of that particular Shaytan.

It is from here Iblis appears to bleed into the Christian Lucifer who through his fall from grace becomes Shaytan or in the Bible Satan the adversary. Whilst Satan the accuser appears in many religious/gnostic texts, there is still just the one mention of Lucifer in Isaiah.

It is not until Christianity slowly began to enter into the Pagan populations that Satan acquires a sex drive and grows horns as he takes on the appearance of several Pagan fertility gods.

Although Lucifer is a Roman name his Pagan origins do not necessarily begin in Rome. The Romans were famous for their love of all things Greek and much of the accepted Roman culture dates to the Greek Hellenistic period including their religious views and pantheon. This includes Lucifer whose Greek counterpart was known as Eosphorous/Phosphorous 'the morning star' and only became Lucifer

on his arrival in Rome. To the Greeks he was the son of Astraeus and Eos (God of the dusk and Goddess of the dawn). His mother Eos is paralleled in the Vedic Sanskrit as 'Ushas' and Latin Aurora both of which are goddesses of dawn. Interestingly the dawn Goddess' siblings include a brother Helios the god of the sun, and a sister Selene the goddess of the moon. This goes some way to explaining the biblical misnomer in Isaiah (the son of the morning) and the subsequent mythos borne out of this misnomer.

His father Astraeus like his mother was one of the Titan Gods, an astrological deity; God of the dusk/evening twilight who with his wife Eos had many sons, the four winds, the five planets including Venus as Eosphoros/Phosphorous–the morning star and Hesperus the evening star.

In fact the only place the name Lucifer really exists is in Roman astronomy as Venus, the morning star which appears in the sky just before dawn, heralding the rising sun. It is a solely Latin name originating from the Latin term lucem ferre, bringer, or bearer, of light.

Adding to the intrigue is the school of thought that perhaps Prometheus and Lucifer are perhaps one and the same...Prometheus meaning forethought is like Eosphorous a Titan who like Yahweh is credited with the creation of man from clay, and who like Satan in the Garden of Eden or Iblis the Djinn defies his gods by in this case giving fire to humanity, an act that enabled progress and civilization, just as Satan gave Adam and Eve the knowledge of good and evil. Unlike Satan, however, Prometheus is known for his intelligence and as a champion of humankind.

Baphomet

It is virtually impossible to talk about Lucifer without at least a brief mention of Baphomet, for if Lucifer is synonymous with the Christian Devil then Baphomet must in some way be synonymous with Lucifer.

After all it is the archetypal image of Baphomet that adorns so many tarot decks as the devil card. The name Baphomet appeared in July 1098 in a letter by the crusader Anselm of Ribemont:

"As the next day dawned, they called loudly upon Baphometh; and we prayed silently in our hearts to God, then we attacked and forced all of them outside the city walls."

This Baphomet became a convenient scapegoat (no pun intended) for the trial by torture of many of the Knights Templar. Over one hundred charges were brought against the Knights Templar the majority of which were the same charges levelled against the Cathars. The indictment (acte d'accusation) published by the court of Rome set forth... "that in all the provinces they had idols, that is to say, heads, some of which had three faces, others but one; sometimes, it was a human skull... That in their assemblies, and especially in their grand chapters, they worshipped the idol as a god, as their saviour, saying that this head could save them, that it bestowed on the order all its wealth, made the trees flower, and the plants of the earth to sprout forth."

Despite the vague descriptions and lack of clear evidence surrounding Baphomet by the end of the 19th century Baphomet acquired new status when Eliphas Lévi, the French occult author and magician who's Dogme et Rituel de la Haute Magie (*Dogmas and Rituals of High Magic*) was published in two volumes (*Dogme*, 1854, *Rituel*, 1856). And inside, he included as the frontispiece an image he had drawn which he described as both Baphomet and "The Sabbatic Goat." It showed a winged human goat with a pair of breasts and a flame between its horns which Lévi described as 'The absolute in symbolic form' which he elaborated on in his description of the frontispiece.

"The goat on the frontispiece carries the sign of the pentagram on the forehead, with one point at the top, a symbol of light, his two hands forming the sign of occultism, the one pointing up to the white moon of

Chesed, the other pointing down to the black one of Geburah. This sign expresses the perfect harmony of mercy with justice. His one arm is female, the other male like the ones of the androgyne of Khunrath, the attributes of which we had to unite with those of our goat because he is one and the same symbol. The flame of intelligence shining between his horns is the magic light of the universal balance, the image of the soul elevated above matter, as the flame, whilst being tied to matter, shines above it. The beast's head expresses the horror of the sinner, whose materially acting, solely responsible part has to bear the punishment exclusively; because the soul is insensitive according to its nature and can only suffer when it materializes. The rod standing instead of genitals symbolizes eternal life, the body covered with scales the water, the semi-circle above it the atmosphere, the feathers following above the volatile. Humanity is represented by the two breasts and the androgyne arms of this sphinx of the occult sciences."

Aleister Crowley, the English occultist stated there was no devil subsequently adopting Lévi's Baphomet as a fertility symbol and the union of opposites. Crowley also developed a theory claiming the name Baphomet referred to the god Mithras and at one point adopted the name Baphomet for himself. This only served to fuel the Christian conviction that Baphomet and the Devil were one and the same. It is easy to see through ritual how Eliphas Lévi's Baphomet came into being.

The hooves of the wild beast, the phallus of Pan, the mercy and severity of the adversary, the fire of the intellect, the wings of the angel, the crescent moon of Thoth, the pentagram all wrapped up in the sacred goat of antiquity.

So who or indeed what is Lucifer and what does it mean to the occultist today?

Lucifer has certainly evolved over the ages and in doing so has come to incorporate many aspects.

He is Cernunnous the horned guardian of the forest who awakens the senses with the deep musky scent of the primordial rage of the wild beast that lives in all of us.

He is the lust of Pan the erotic piper whose seductive tune and fertile imagination drives creation.

He is Prometheus, fire of the intellect who champions progress and science.

He is Iblis the controversial who is always true to self...the fool who follows the path of the heart.

He is Satanael the adversary who never blindly accepts without questioning first, the rebel who is not afraid to speak his mind.

He is Thoth the wisdom and understanding of the ages.

Whatever name you know him as Lucifer is there waiting for all those who seek enlightenment and who are constantly driven by the tantalising flicker of Prometheus' fire and the illuminating flame of Lucifer's light in those rare moments of clarity.

– Lucifer –

Child that followed the dance,
Of the morning star,
Bathed in light and
Baptised with fire.

It is impossible to say whether or not any of this was initially borne out of ritual or something much deeper, and indeed if it was the result of a ritual...whose ritual! Either way this was my earliest experience of astral projection. And it was within the astral mists that my visions and dreams took shape.

There are no boundaries in the world of a child, it is a time when life is an uncomplicated web of possibilities. It is only when we look

through the eyes of adulthood that the mystical world of a child enters the realms of fantasy and we no longer see the truth! As a small child I would regularly experience clairaudience, hearing familiar voices not unlike that of my Mother, initially these occurred as I drifted on the threshold of sleep. It was from the stillness of my dreams that I first saw tantalising glimpses of the light that would lead me through the world of magick.

It was in those hazy realms of hypnagogia I could feel myself floating and become aware that I am able to transcend the confines of my physical world. On the edge of sleep visions and hallucinations are a common reality and it is here that I discover there is another world beyond the bedroom wall…A world of magick where the limits and constraints of the material world cease to exist. My most vivid and recurring vision or dream features an ancient cave with paintings on the wall, where the warm glow of the firelight flickers across ancient shadows. It is here that I first encounter the horned figure who although animalistic has a beauty which captivates my imagination and I realise that he like many later astral encounters transcends the spoken word, communicating through silence like Aleister Crowley's Aiwass or John Dee's Pure Verities. It is within this silence although young I am aware of an ancient truth that through time I will come to understand is born out of the chaos of creation.

As a child I have many recurring dreams where I am sat in silence as an observer. I am sure there were many visions and dreams which I experienced but in the most memorable I am watching as the blood drips from the throats of two sacrificial white and the black fowl that only moments earlier pecked the ground.

He offers me the chalice and I drink from it.

Although I was only a young child, I was drawn to this teacher of the magickal artes who resides in the astral mists. I know there is more and although I am hungry for knowledge I was far too young to fully

understand and so for a while I had to be content to drift in and out of this magickal world through the dreams and the visions that live on the edge of sleep. Yet with every sip I became more intoxicated and my hunger for knowledge grew stronger.

By the time I was seven years old I began to learn of the polytheistic world of the ancient Greeks and Romans seeing many images that were similar to the horned figure of my dreams and although I did not know it he had already begun to shape my world.

As I grew my conscious world facilitated my spiritual growth through the myths and legends of the ancient Gods, totem animals (most often the leopard) which in my childish brain walked beside me reminiscent of the demons in *The Golden Compass* and the macabre fairy tales of writers such as the brothers Grimm.

Like all young children and especially young girls I was passionate, but while other girls raved about horses, pop stars, boyfriends and platform shoes, I longed for the magick of the witch, dragons and all that the ethereal world could offer fuelling my passions through the written word as I began to write poetry and short stories. Later my interest would be captivated by ghost stories and the macabre world of the Vampyre. I would often look out of my bedroom window in the early hours of the morning and wonder at the dark world of frost covered twilight just before the dawn when the morning star shines brightest.

I was enthralled by the world of the Vampyre that lived within the shadows, but unlike my contemporaries I did not see the Vampyre as someone un-dead who preyed on the weak and tainted all they touched like the Gothic blood suckers of Hollywood horror films whose pseudo eroticism bordered on the profane. My Vampyres were something more captivating who, while they could be just as merciless, even to a teenager their cruelty bordered on the world of magick. As I crossed the threshold into womanhood I left behind the simple world of the

child and with it my understanding of Vampyres as they became a metaphor for those who by drinking the blood of life satiated their inner dragon.

Like all children I grew older and as I did so the more I understood and the more hungry I became for that knowledge which he offered. I could feel him growing ever closer as I fed that hunger with Omar Khayam, Mary Shelly, Bram Stoker, Cheiro, in fact anything that would satisfy my appetite for the occult and the macabre.

Like many of my peers a fire burned within me that raged through my teenage years which I doused with the angry poetry and vivid imagery of punk rock. I frequented the places that would feed my hungry mind, drinking in the heavy aggressive atmospheres of the time. It is only now when I look back that I realise my trashy appearance and aggressive music choice afforded me a way of expressing the fire, the hunger, the desire–the dragon that raged inside me waiting to understand, to be satiated–always waiting.

In the post-childhood world I stand alone as I make the transition from Maiden to Mother. I can feel his presence but it is changed and I am powerless, yielding to his strength as he leads the dance of my life. He calls me to experience and indulge all my senses as I feast at the table of Dionysis and Lilith, plunging deeper and deeper into the dark recesses of my being for only in darkness will I seek the light.

I experience all that I need seeking sacrilegious solace in the lustful gaze of the beautiful, desperate and profane. Relationships cannot survive beyond my own primitive lust as free from any moral constraints and unaware of why I ride the beast. I do not feel love in the same way, nor do I wish to. I am in awe of the daemon that leads the dance and I am drawn constantly to him in a way that leaves no room for the complications of the emotional ties between earthly lovers.

The element of fear which has been introduced by the indoctrination of mainstream religion taught in school, is far outweighed by the

excitement, passion and devotion for Lucifer and all that lay ahead of me as I follow his labyrinthine path where fear and desire are intertwined and the morning star lights the way.

> *I traverse this universe*
> *Through castles made of sand*
> *The fool that walks behind the Mage*
> *And seeks to understand*

These are the wilderness years where life plunges me into a desolate void where there is no light or dark just emptiness. They say what doesn't kill you makes you stronger and I had dived head first into a world of purgatory where violence, addiction, pain and loss were commonplace. The world of the adult was a stark contrast to the simplicity of my happy childhood. The unconditional love a mother feels for her children is a far cry from the lustful desires of the rebellious teenager. During these years I felt fear, anger, sorrow, pain, grief and eventually heartbreak. I was a mother, a wife and a witch.

As an adult with a violent drunk for a husband and four children it was easy to feel lost. Worse than that there were times of darkness, but this darkness was different to the macabre gothic darkness of my youth. This darkness was heavy and oppressive, so with my hands outstretched I reach for him, I call to him moreover I long for him. I need to feel his touch, to sense his eyes burning into me. I am aching. I am hungry and I am lost. I am consumed by the mundane, lost in an empty chasm where nothing can touch me. There are many roads on Lucifer's path and this was one where pain and loss go hand in hand. The path of the magician is not an easy one and can make many demands–mental, physical and emotional.

This was a time of questioning and I sought many routes to find my way back, honing my skills with many adept teachers some of which

were less aware of the part they played in my life. Not all of which were mystics, mediums or even spiritual...If you need to learn how to bathe the baby then the midwife is adept!!

During these lost years I stared addiction in the face, if not my own then that of my partners and later even my children. I experienced the agonising heartache of losing not one but two children. And having divorced the father of all my children who had lost all control over his life, long before I met him, I moved on, re-marrying someone just as problematic. This too culminated in divorce. The world seemed cold and austere. I am tired and becoming overpowered by a sense of hopelessness, lost in the shadows and screaming for the light to guide me.

It was around this time I recall watching the film *The Ninth Gate* and it only took one line from that film to awaken all that had lain dormant for far too long.

"I saw him one day. I was fifteen years old, and I saw him as plain as I see you now: cutaway, top hat, cane–Very elegant, very handsome. It was love at first sight."

It may not have been my recollection but it was enough to rekindle the fire. These weren't lost years at all. Lucifer has many aspects and teaches many lessons. I emerged older, wiser and stronger. I had learned to fight...I was a warrior, I had learned to take responsibility and I had an inner strength that would carry me through many difficult times, I had learned to love unconditionally and I had learned to forgive. I was older, wiser and the fire within burned stronger than ever.

> *I danced naked with the morning star*
> *A dance of defiance and rapture and awe*
> *The light that guides the mage*
> *And clarifies all that we are*

The following version of the middle pillar is borne out of ritual...

Lucifer is the light of creation, the warm breath of the fire serpent that brings inspiration and clarity. He is both organic and orgasmic and I am flesh and I eat from the earthly table of desire as I long for the warmth of the fire and the light of inspiration that I seek through desire. I am hungry for all that seduces, awakens my senses and fuels my own lust and desire for ultimately that is what leads me to the light of Lucifer.

In the darkness I hear him as he beckons me to feel his presence and though I feel powerless to resist I know that my surrender is power in itself. He calls me to him and my lust hears and responds through the ritual of desire, touch and the energy of sexual arousal...this is tantric... this is sex magick!

By focusing your breathing into the Chakras that form the Kundalini or Fire Serpent it is possible to know and eventually invoke the energy known as Lucifer in many of his various guises yet initially I am unsure what to expect as I feel the energy rise up my spine.

I breathe into the Root Chakra and I almost instantly become aware of him. I hear him call to me, "Know me as Cernunnous the sorcerer of ages past, the shaman in the caves of Ariège, the horned guardian of the forest who awakens the senses with the deep musky scent of the wild beast for I am all that is primordial. I am the hunter whose stealth and cunning nourishes the hungry mind and feeds the lustful soul, I am the wild rage that burns in you, I am all that cannot be tamed... Know me on the tree of life in Malkuth–The Earthly Kingdom where I am the Lord of all beasts and the ruler of life, death and rebirth.

Drawing upwards into the Sacral Chakra and allowing the energy to flow freely up the spine know me as Pan, I am all that you desire, all that you lust after, I am the sexual attraction you feel towards another, the hauntingly erotic piper that seduces the senses, I am the energy that drives creation...Feel me as the passionate heart that beats ever stronger. I am the lecherous fantasy of the smouldering beauty that

captures the imagination. I come to you in your dreams and it is my scent that disturbs your sleep. Know me in Yesod–The Foundation of all life, for I am Lord of Arcadia, the fertile ground that ensures the continuation of life.

As the energy rises to the Naval Chakra know me as Prometheus, the fire of defiance, here you will feel the strength of the warrior, for I will not blindly accept my fate but will fight for progress and champion science, I am the stealth of the mercenary, the last tear of the hero and the glory of the victor....I am the fight that will not be silenced, I am the rebel, the martyr and the suffragette...I am progress. Know me in Hod and Netzach–The Glory and the Victory, the fire and the intellect that drives the brave.

Breathing into the Heart Chakra know me as Iblis, although I am controversial, I am always true to self. I am the fire elemental that will not be suppressed and cannot be silenced, I am the fool who follows the path of the heart, the perfect lover whose loyalty is unyielding. I am the true will that drives the creative emotion of love. I am the despair of the failed hellequin...On the tree of life know me in Tifareth–Where 'Do what thou wilt shall be the whole of the Law...Love is the law, love under will.'

At the Throat Chakra know me as Satanael. I am the adversary who never blindly accepts without questioning first, the rebel who is not afraid to speak his mind. I know right from wrong and I weigh the heart and challenge all...On the tree of life know me in Geburah and Chesed–For I am the devil's advocate and I speak with both Severity and Mercy.

I will lead you through Daath where the questioning nature of Satanael points the way to the realm of Thoth where the balance of good and evil is maintained through the intellect.

At the Third Eye Chakra know me as Thoth. Born of the intellect I am both philosopher and magician. I am the scientist and the poet; the

In Honour of the Lightbearers by Geraldine Lambert

alchemist and scribe whose divine intelligence maintains the balance of universal energies. I am the wisdom of the peacekeeper that ends wars and champions justice. I am the wisdom of the ages, the moon child who lights the darkness....On the tree of life know me in Chokmah and Binah–For I am both Wisdom and Understanding.

At the Crown Chakra know me for I am Lucifer, the bringer of light, the Morning star, the first light. I am the divine light of creation, through me is communion with all that has ever been, I open the door to the realms beyond for I am the shining light of the astral world. I am the hermit of the abyss who illuminates the path. I am the silvery glow of moonlight upon your skin as you embrace the path of the witch. Feel me, ever close for I am the fire and the blood of eternal life. I am all you will ever desire because I am your desire...On the tree of life know me in Kether as I am the Crown of Enlightenment.

It is possible through this ritual to discover many other aspects of Lucifer–Lumiel, Lucifuge, Baphomet to name but a few.

Much can be learned through this ritual and how much is dependant as with most things upon the individual. It is designed to understand Lucifer in the context of ritual magick. The aspects of Lucifer in their various forms can be focused upon according to the individual's requirements.

Methods of enhancing this ritual include the use of candles, oils, incense, and music. Of course ritual masturbation or sexual acts ultimately have the most effect. Training your breathing is imperative and will pay later–deep slow breaths taken in through the nose and down into the abdomen before being exhaled slowly through the mouth. Used alongside these other techniques, sexual climax is the most beneficial and ritual masturbation is certainly the best route to begin with. In order to achieve the greatest results the breath is drawn up through the Chakras while further raising the magickal energy through self-stimulation. Initially learning to channel the sexual climax

away from the genitals and up the spine through the Chakras will require practice but once achieved will heighten awareness.

Ritual masturbation is the technique of directing the energy produced by sexual climax up the spine in order to awaken the kundalini energy for the purpose of communion with beings and energies from beyond this world. This is also the safest technique, as any sexual union requires serious consideration, unlike our predecessors we live in a world where sexually transmitted disease brings a new very real set of issues. Where once temple prostitutes were free to practice ritual sex with the mingling of sexual fluids, we live in a world where barrier contraception prevents this occurring. Therefore unless you are fortunate enough for your priest to be your regular partner alternative methods must be considered.

In this instance the ritual masturbation of both Priest and Priestess, representative of the Shakti/Shiva energy, becomes a symbolic ritual sex act on the astral planes. Where possible the joint burning of these fluids can be made as an offering. This form of tantric ritual works well as much magick takes place upon the astral. The above Invocation of Lucifer may also be useful to those seeking a Priest to work with although this is a potent energy and over time women who work with Lucifer may find it is easier and indeed equally effective to visualise themselves as his lover. As I said this is a powerful energy which for me is a devotional path, although I do not view myself as Luciferian as that tends to imply that I adhere to the dogma and practices associated with Luciferianism which I do not. My relationship with Lucifer is in a spiritual, non-religious form that has no specific creed and therefore my devotion is freely given.

Usually the link between Priest and Priestess is a form of sacred love and the bond between them is unbreakable, but for women who work with Lucifer it is the bond between Priestess and Lucifer which is unbreakable. This is important as lovers can often appear to take on

the role of Lucifer when required or even desired thereby reducing the need of a Priest although I hasten to add that an experienced Priest will always be beneficial.

Lucifer; powerful, enigmatic and desirable but not for the faint hearted!

– Lucifers Child –

In the fires of eternal light,
The spirit of chaos smiled,
And my immortal soul
Was forged,
For I...Am Lucifers child.

And I am all that is raw,
Primordial and wild,
One who cannot
Be tamed,
For I...Am Lucifers child.

I will dance with spirits,
Just for a little while,
Between the realms of
Life and death,
For I...Am Lucifers child.

A truly acquired taste,
Pure eloquence and style,
Understood by
So very few,
For I...Am Lucifers child.

Both my enemy and my friend,
I will charm and beguile,
Mystify,
And confound,
For I...Am Lucifers child.

But when I am afraid,
Alone or feeling fragile,
It is hardest
To remember,
That I...Am Lucifers child.

Lucifers Child by Semirani Vine

References

Bible KJV
The Latin Vulgate
Strong's Concordance H1966
The Holy Q'uran
The Theogony of Hesiod

Calvin, John (2007), *Commentary on Isaiah*, 1:404. Translated by John King, Charleston, SC, Forgotten Books.

Daniell, David (2003), *The Bible in English: Its History and Influence*, New Haven, CT, Yale University Press, ISBN 0-300-09930-4.

Day, John (2002), *Yahweh and the Gods and Goddesses of Canaan*, Continuum International Publishing Group, ISBN 0-82646830-6, ISBN 978-0-8264-6830-7.

Boyd, Gregory A. (1997), *God at War: The Bible and Spiritual Conflict*, InterVarsity Press, ISBN: 0-8308-1885-5, ISBN: 978-0-8308-1885-3.

Smith, Gary V., (30 August 2007), *The New American Commentary: Isaiah 1-39, Vol. 15A*, B&H Publishing Group, ISBN 978-0-80540115-8.

Beeks, R. S. P. (2009), *Etymological Dictionary of Greek*, Brill, ISBN: 9789004174184.

Barber, Malcolm; Bate, Keith (2010), *Letters from the East: Crusaders, Pilgrims and Settlers in the 12th-13th Centuries*, Ashgate

Publishing, ISBN 978-0-7546-6356-0.

Complete Translation of "Dogme Et Rituel De La Haute Magie" With A Biographical Preface By Arthur Edward Waite, ISBN: 978-1-108-06216-9

Michelet, Jules, *History of France, Volume 1*, ASIN: B005GE3BAQ.

Babalon and the Beast
Art and Poem by Lorraine Sherwin

Astride or infront
Nuit like
Offering the Star kiss
Bring waves of Bliss
A hurricane of light
The Serpent takes flight
Ingorging the Spheres in Her Path
A Unison of Old
The Star-Seed unfolds
Like a Lotus flower
Guttering Molten Gold

Sexual Magick: Point to Point

by Charlotte Rodgers

As far back as I can remember, my world view has been that of an animist who believes that magic is inherent and natural to everything, whether it is worked with or not.

Living in New Zealand in the 1970's and 1980's there was little information available on esoteric subjects. I hunted down what I could, studied and filtered it, and eventually gravitated towards the work of Aleister Crowley which I merged into a personalised chaotic amalgamation of techniques and traditions. All of the approaches that appealed to me incorporated some form of the harnessing of sexual energy; something which I acknowledged easily as having power but never fully explored at that time. In hindsight this seems such a waste as during the high and hormonal early years of my life I loved hard and intensely, was very promiscuous and worked in the sex industry, so could have had incredibly interesting sexual magickal adventures. However I was mad as a brush and a latent sensible side, thankfully, held me back.

In my early thirties I was stable enough to take the risks that intense magickal explorations can posit and I started using sex consciously in ritual, venturing beyond the utilisation of energy from masturbation which had been a mainstay in my practice for a long, long time.

Orgasm from masturbation I have always used extensively; not just

in the charging of sigils, but also as a way to aid astral projection, implanting myself in someone else's head space, and to send messages and commune with various spirit and god forms that I work with.

Before I continue I think that I should clarify what I mean by sex magick. In my mind it is magick that incorporates the whole self, and this goes beyond gender. I can see why some people have issues with the necessity of a male/female polarity but in my mind gender is a box of a definition that shows the limitations of man, not the gods.

In my own work, the more I opened my mind, the less defining the concept of gender became and the influence of moon phases became an obvious part of how I viewed sexual delineations, in that at various aspects of the moon my mind was more likely to encompass and translate according to certain genders. Thus at full moon my mind was more female orientated, new moon male, and at the dark moon my mind was open to impressions that were alien to its conditioning and education.

Ironically pushing through these barriers created a comfort with my own sexuality causing it to shift from bisexual to heterosexual to celibate, which amongst some of my, open minded to the point of being narrow minded, peers was considered deviant and close minded.

It's all about love pure and simple, love and self.

Anyway, that digression aside, sexual magick being about the true self, it necessarily explores all emissions from the body. Blood, breast milk, ejaculates, and waste products.

I found very little in the way of applicable and practical textual assistance which seemed strange in a spiritual practice that acknowledges that the body is an essential part of our whole, and is therefore a vital working tool, in itself.

I found it difficult to access support from other female practitioners which was frustrating until I realised that especially within the Thelemic community, women are rare and therefore may perceive

themselves as having more power by being aloof from others of their sex. (I came to this realisation not just through analysis of others but by analysis of myself by the way).

This sort of practice is also very iconoclastic and can create judgements, so women necessarily are discrete especially if they have a family, children and are in the mainstream public eye in any way.

I felt at times that there was little interest in really pushing boundaries for women in this area and I came to believe that many traditions are much more conservative than I had previously thought; not conservative because that was their essential nature but conservative because they were hidebound by traditions and book learning and often used this as a way to stall progression; be silent and keep the power to yourself or in some cases, disguise the fact that there is no real power.

I encountered groups that experimented with sex magick in a way that made me very uncomfortable and struck me as being abusive, and more about exploitation and power games than spiritual adventuring. These judgements on my part caused personal analysis of my own morality, however, and I concur that there are private and very sound groups that do this sort of work but that there are also people and groups that use sexual magick as a cover for actions that are motivated by nothing more than sexual gratification at the expense of others.

It became clear that the onus was on my own focused determination to explore this realm. I found several books of value such as Mishlen Linden's *Typhonian Terotomas* and *Sexual Magick* by Mogg Morgan; connected up with a few maverick male magickians who supported women's work, co-founded a discussion group with others of a similar inclination, started a correspondence with the editor of this anthology, Mishlen Linden, and began.

I started with in-depth explorations of my menstrual cycle and venous blood work which led to many revelations on my relationships

with the worlds around me.

Food and fuel.

I also loved deeply and whilst I used orgasms within relationships with other magicians' to take me places, at that time my primary goal was using sexual energy to explore my relationship with myself and the spheres that I operate in and with.

My having hep c did change the nature of some of this work. Using condoms is easily enough integrated into one's practice, making the act even more deliberate and mindful. I would have been uncomfortable with working with a partner that I didn't know well and trusted implicitly which made the rituals more powerful.

I had intercourse with earthenware urns, God Forms and Magisters of groups that had an initiatory prerequisite of sodomy. I had magickal sex with my tattooist who utilised a traditional Japanese tattooing technique and was inside me as he inked a charged sigil into my skin.

I qualified as a yoga practitioner and I incorporated breath work and asana in my explorations. I pushed boundaries and moved through elations and chaos and depression.

I learned a lot. I learned about power and I learned about the danger of relationships with otherworldly beings that seem to be more important, real and relevant than the people that inhabit this world.

I learned that sex magick has transformative power, yes, but it is Love that really holds the ability to effect true change and create realisations and revelations.

When I passed through menopause things shifted and my relationship with myself became deeper and more profound.

I realised that just as blood holds power, so does the absence of it. As I moved beyond being defined by my ability to bleed and bear, my love of myself became greater.

Yes, my use of sex magick has changed me and has enhanced my life.

Sex and sexuality is who we are; working with that energy is

learning about ourselves and our relationship with everything around us.

Sure, it gets things done, but doing isn't the greatest magick; knowing, being, directing and loving are.

True Magick does Not Exist Without True Love.

Lilith by Mishlen Linden

In the Garden of Earthly Delights
From the Magickal Record of Mishlen Linden

Building the Body of Babalon

Our sacred bodies hold the keys to the Temple of Secrets and we are all given the tools we need to rise above ourselves, to gaze upon the infinite. In the final analysis, we get what we give....we should leave something in there...in that dark warmth of Being, that cradle of life and love, where the heart glides with passion into the Other.

Oneness is achieved in fullest ecstasy...what place is this? What fullness of joy is achieved? Given into and exhausted, desire is lost to our body, but is the gift lost also?

If so, then it was never truly given.

Repelling up another's chakras is a difficult task, one needs spiritual muscles to push from one chakra up into another. Therefore practice gradually goes a bit farther and stays awhile. Learn to control this and the next step will eventually call to you...arising, a new world is gained. With spiritual muscles flexed by practice and use, one gradually attains the abilities to move to the next rung; keep rising–there is no end except for the one we create for our Selves.

We Priestesses all may come from different traditions, but one thing we all share are the energetic sources of our bodies. These chakras,

whether we are young or old all come from the same cosmic source that gives life to our being. These are the roots to our Body of Babalon. From our bodies does this sacred force come. It is this energy which gives us the sacred capability to build our priestess body. Decide who and what is the "real you," your empowered self. Skeletal to voluptuous, dark to light, shining or a gulf of blackness, there is no threshold you can not cross. Are you human? Are you part animal, or alien? Are your breasts like volcanos? They can emit elixirs–one red, one white; these your priest can drink from.

You can create more than one self. It is a crafting of a vessel to voyage afar. All of the power is within and without you to change your Selves as you Will. When you have decided on what your body is to be,

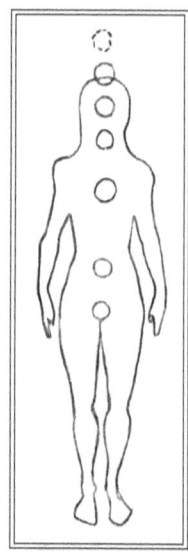

The Chakras

tell your priest. You will also be using his Seeing to feed your Image. It connects the circuit between you, the give and take necessary for all Magick. Your Self, His Self, and the free energy around you creates its own Triangle of Manifestation.

These notes come from my magickal record. As such, they do not always progress in a linear fashion. Other forces creep in and are assuaged or banished. One's life does not progress in a linear fashion- it progresses in a NATURAL fashion. And Nature is a work of Art, and Art, as we all know, is Magick.

In the reading, you may find differing views that contradict one another. Choose the one which resonates with you, and then create your own.

The Time for Self-Initiation Has Come

Entice yourself until your kalas flow...dip your index finger into

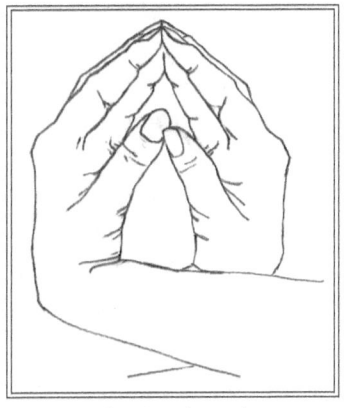

The Pearl Mudra

your yoni and bring it forth. Draw upon your heart "The Sigil of Babalon." Repeat over and over, until you see and feel its brightness. Make the mudra of The Pearl before you. The Pearl is made as follows: at your heart center, cross right hand/wrist over the left, and form a cup with your hands, bringing fingertips and thumb tips together. There will be an open space between your palms. This is done right up against your heart chakra. It is not easy, and its best to practice this beforehand. In use, the air between your palms will begin to glow golden, and it is THIS that is The Pearl. The Pearl can also be used for centering during traumatic times, for it is a healing energy as well.

- Speak -

These are my gifts:
I command the Earth, sacred vessel of my Bodies Light.
I command the Waters, on ancient seas flowing, kalas
of life from within my Womb.
I command the Air, which fills my body with Life.
I command the Fires, which blaze within my Heart.
For I am She: Babalon, Shakti, initiator!
Doorway to the Path of Self-Knowledge
And Priestess of Transformation!

Feel the power inside you. Sit and be within it in contemplation of the Holy Divine. Learn to be comfortable within your awakened body.

Your Priest

And now it's time to find your Priest. He will embody the Divine Design within us all. He does not need to be an Adept, but one who has the ability to become an Adept. He must have the most sacred ability to recognize and honor Adepthood, within you and within himself. He needs the skill/talent of visualization, and be able to clear his body and mind of the mental litter of the day. An ideal priest will need to be sensitive to your own energies; as fearless as yourself. His heart will need to be open to yours, as well as open to trance vision. You may already have a Priest, then the searching would not be necessary.

Do not be concerned about his appearance. This is not what you are working with. You are working with his divine spirit, and he, with yours. Remember this!

Scanning him, you might find grey or brownish grey spots in his aura. You may want to work on healing these places within him. He should learn to wield his body's energies as one would an essential instrument of power–with precision, one-pointed focus and control. Just as you will need to wield your body's energies!

It is helpful for him to share the same magickal system as your own, but not as necessary as you might think. Gods and Goddesses, spirits and loa, all interweave within the unseen, and interact in curious ways.

– Calling the Priest –

As Babalon
I seek the Beast
My hunger to fulfill
The Void which lies within
Silent and deep, but never still.

As Babalon
I ride the waves

*Of ecstasy and desire
It's not for love or passion
But comm-union I desire.*

*As Babalon
I am the eternal warrior
And the eternal whore
And the witch that rides the Beast
Dark, Primordial and Raw.*

Call him In Your Name. Call him from your Sacred Heart. Priest, Lover, Chaos....Become a red rose and open the sacral chakra. Open your red petals, one by one, and exhale your perfume out into the astral aires.

Become brighter and brighter, and feel the space around you, until you sense his Presence, human or Other. Entice him to follow your scent. Flirt with Love, Dance and Chaos. Become One with him, drawing him ever closer to your scent.[1]

Repeat this ritual until he comes to you. You may enhance it with ritual masturbation. If he hasn't come, look upon all those around you with your magickal eyes. Look again. For you may not have noticed him. He may have been in your life all this time, unrecognized. There may be an electromagnetic jump between you when you look into his eyes after this rite. He should recognize you as well, for you have created the sacred bridge between the two of you. Now it is ready to be walked.

My Beloved had died. In many years together, and years apart, we woke ourselves to the ancient art of bliss. Joy came through our bodies, and we used its power. We traveled distant realms. There, we were always together. Now our work can only be done through the paths we once traveled. That exploration required our bodies. That limited our

---

[1] *Calling the Priest* and the above two paragraphs co-written with Diane Narraway.

magicks as well as well as our exploration. He stands in ashes at my bedside, and our magick now is only one of memory.

I bring this up because we have feelings, we all have the need to be loved, and sexual tantra walks a very tight rope. There is a great danger of identifying the magick with the man (or woman). All of us carry the seeds of love, and of a Greater Love. The work we do is skillful as a surgeon, much closer than human love. Our work can create an illusion–and it is as much of a danger to your partner as it is to you–that he is the One Source that opens the Greater Doors of inner mastery. And he can be–but to take him as so you must give up the title of Babalon, as She loves all. Babalon does not fall into this "one source" delusion.

On the outer Babalon is the Sacred Whore and she appears and acts as the Sacred Whore. She is not addicted to any one person. Falling in love is just that–Falling. The partner becomes the Man of Earth that nature intended in order to extend our species, and those are the energies she and her partner will have access to. It is a beautiful, predictable rhythm. But by keeping the relationship of the energy body actively empowered and dedicated to that which lies beyond, the forces around us are free to enter, change, metamorphose into a greater being. And to do that, we must sacrifice a precious belonging: that of personal love. This is the sacrifice of Babalon.

Then I stood alone after my Beloved died. There was naught to do but wander, waiting for my body to die. My spirit withered, my chakras dimmed in mourning. Then a Voice spoke: Call upon Lakshmi. I had worked with her in the past, and we had worked well together. She is a woman, and she knows our challenges. With her help lies the hope that perhaps my heart could be eased, though never without sorrow. There is no end to grief, but there is an eternal path in which love can rise again. She guides us to it.

There were other tasks to complete. Work to do. I knew I could find another even in my diminished body, a man who could revive my energy body. At that time, it was all that I wanted. I did not know of the greater task that lay before me.

My spiritual teacher was participating in a Sundance ritual at the time. He had said that he would pray for me, while he was there. The powers of the Sundance came to me in the form of awakened awareness of that timeless "spark" of the divine which is in each of us. It was not old, it was not young. It simply was. And I began to see it in everyone around me...

It was then that Lakshmi spoke: Find him online, she said. No need to light candles and perform incantations, she is up to date on her tech!

And so I did.

Or, actually, he found me. He was 28 years old, and I am 58, but the spark, as I said before, is timeless. Nor does it take notice of size, shape, form or color. His Goddess, Hecate, had told him that he would find an older woman to work with. That he would learn from her. At first, I demurred. But he continued his requests. I said to myself "Lakshmi wouldn't send a man that young"...still he said that he was the one. I saw that "spark" within him, as well. Slowly I became interested. He had a rare quality of respect—a sense of the sacred. The sense of the sacred must be recognized! Without that awareness, you will never awake the connection to the higher selves within.

Those most sure of their greatness are those who are least likely to have it. But he wanted to learn. He showed me the respect due to those of my vocation. Respect is essential, and if you don't have it from the beginning, it will not form later. It is like water to a seed. And I needed to re-build my body of light. He was a message of hope, and I will call him A, my priest.

We the priestesses control our chakras. Our yoni, our vesica, in

symbol comes anciently from the mark for fish. And fish is what lives in the sea of life, the sea we all emerged from. It is as surely one of our eyes, our Ayin, the yoni-eye, as are the two of Malkuth, or the one set above them, commonly called our Third Eye, or the Ajna chakra.

Our priest has his own eye, his own Ayin, which penetrates us. Like a hexagram, we share common ground. Crowley attributes the Hebrew letter Ayin, to the Devil in his and Freda Harris' Thoth Tarot Deck. Hence a warning–do not be chained by your desire. We are here to serve, not to accumulate power.

We both needed healing badly. He was damaged by a failed marriage. So first we began by re-building our chakras together, re-awakening our inner Light. I found myself an eye agate–an agate which has been cut in such a way that it looks like an eye. These agates are stones of earthing, and the eye–appropriate for the Yoni, the region with which we are working.

I put it inside of me. During each ritual to come, it is there, soaking in the kalas. Agates are permeable. On the market they are often dyed. I shall permeate it with my own kalas, and will keep it on my altar between-times.

Magickal Record

– July 14, 2013 –

It is a simple matter to drift into the arms of the Other...don't stop it...it is natural and what we would do if not for the artificial laws we have created that keep us apart. I see his body, filled with the nerves one would see in an Alex Grey painting. I see my own, and I pull him down into me...sex...the red light pulses with desire. I wrap my nerves around him, I take him inside me...I am all hunger for him...devour him

whole...so good, I feel like this consummation makes me whole. We sit asana, and I wrap my arms about him, pushing. This is sex. This is where most people leave the energy.

The first thing I learn is that Cuming is the end of it. So don't let him cum, keep him as hungry as you are...stay in that state of desire for as long as you can. That is the first ability that must be learned. Without it, the rest won't happen. I devour him slowly. I take more and more of him. I am a starving woman with an endless appetite, and I do not cum...must not...for as long as I can, for as long as he can. It is dark all around us–we light up our universe, we make up our universe, we ARE our universe. To go on to orgasm is the grounding of the current, so stay here, stay here forever....until the burst of white light destroys All...

– July 17 –

If a man can be likened to a serpent, then a woman can be likened to a spider...we draw them into our web and await them...

A and I create our temple of darkness...the only light is a glowing computer screen casting blue and white light around us. No candles necessary! Desire swells our organs, he is inside me and our hands are extended and they touch, palm to palm...my fingers leave trails and I wrap these trails around his, we are tied together with each others light.

They glow white, then golden..and lifeforce flows up our arms, into our hearts. Our sex continues...the pulse red, but now the energy is sharing itself in our palms, in our arms, in our solar plexus, and it is easier to control, there is a balance to our life force now...we have gone from making a point, to making a line...the channel begins to emerge from our bodies.

Next to the bed is my Beloved's altar. I had wondered how he would react–he had been very jealous in the past. But now he is filled with

lechery, desire of his own—he wanted part of what we had. I allow him to take part of me, and that seems to satisfy his craving. It was a small part of the entire world of light that was being created around A and me.

Gold, gold, bright gold...as it passes through my fingers, palms, up to my shoulders and lo! My arms become wings! Golden wings of light...I become Isis!!...is this part of my Beloved's magick? For he was based in the Egyptian current. And he had remained with me, focusing himself on his altar, that had his ashes, his art, his sacred book—*Osiris Awakened* with his hair on it. And his candle, although it was not lit. I had become Black Isis at his funeral wake. But now I am a Golden Isis, filled with love.

And I was with my Priest, and he was alive.

I raise my head and I spread my wings out, around him, and cover him in protection and love. I press him to my heart. I become Nurture, another goddess, and they are One. And another awareness flickers inside of me...an image by the Pre-Raphaelite artist Edward Robert Hughes...a painting of the goddess of death, carrying A away...my self-consciousness fades, and my priest tells me that he has just had a heart orgasm. It seems that each chakra has a different, unique kind of orgasm...what a lovely thing to share.

So I learn, there is a different kind of orgasm from each of the chakras...I love what I am learning...and decide I should begin writing everything in detail, lest it be lost. This is what we started to heal ourselves, but many other things are coming to us in the process.

No, this should not be lost.

– July 18 –

It is afternoon when we meet, unexpectedly. Desire wells up out of nowhere, takes both of us in its grasp. We sit yab-yum, and he

puts himself into me. We begin breathing each others air. Far more than air is exchanged by this...in come the particles of being, of life, in come the darknesses kept inside...this air is, after all, coming from our lungs, located around our hearts. It is distinct from kissing...the act of kissing can draw in each others chemicals, in a worldly manner. This is somehow purer (not better, just different) as the subtle unseen force is not interfered with, or concealed by the hardness of a wet sucking mouth, sharing hormones and desire.

Our bodies move closer, and I put my forehead upon his. Our Ajna chakras open to each other. Mine looks like a sideways eye, but I see his differently. It is round and in all the colors of the Tibetan syllable Lha, representing the primordial state of mind. The colors lie like this: the outer color is deep blue, then green, then red, then yellow, then in the center, white. My priest doesn't work within the Tibetan pantheon. I will have to look into this.

But now we have two points of connection, two points of flowing into each other then out of each other, passing light, passing essence. This has formed a circuit, our desire, our three eyes, moving our life force though as our breath exchanges our other, subtle light. We hold our palms towards each others, and they glow, and our bodies are drawn into one another's fully...we are inside each other. Love! Is this a form of love? Or is this self-love?

We pulse together. The intensity grows and I flex my kegal muscles around him to pull him deeper, ever deeper...

And then—climax! At that very moment, my Beloved appeared! While A came, I gave my portion of the energy to my Love...that is why he is not jealous, I realize, he wants that energy...and I realize he is using it to live within me. I need to do this, or he will fade...I poured it into his jar of ashes.

I need to think this through. Death is a complicated process.

– July 25 –

A day needed for more healing...we merge into each other...we love each other...the golden wings, streaked with rainbows, and formed out of our Desire. Now we both had them...with these we covered each other, not being bound by the rules of Malkuth where two things can't inhabit the same place. This has become our Healing ritual. He sees me as an incarnation of Hekate, while I see myself as Nepthys, yet I believe we are giving names to the same Force, and perhaps it is neither. As we repeat this ritual, it grows ever stronger, and ever more automatic. We are creating a ground that is stable, a place of refuge for each other. This becomes our inner Temple. By repeating this, we make astral imprints that will last for as long as we need them.

It would be impossible to do this without sincere love and trust. Be sure of your priest! If you aren't sure of him ask your gods to choose for you.

– July 28 –

We are careful not to touch. The energies have become so subtle that our awareness of them would be tainted, or hidden by the physical. Yet we stand in uninterrupted energetic union on the astral while I am spread-eagled on the bed. My hands are lain palms out, and I burn them white with energy, at the same time both flowing into his hands, and yet also channeling this into my breast. There glows the yellow light of love we have been working with. The sexual frenzy is balanced by these other energies, and it is easier not to draw all of it into my womb. As we lay upon each other astrally, we circulate this life force through each other.

"Like making love to Love." he whispers.

I am earth, he rains down the stars at night, this pure energy...I put my hands over my head, flowing the power into the chakras that

extend over the head. I am not familiar with them, they are above the crown, but I can feel them above me. This is the most important asana I have learned yet. There are five chakras above us, and each brings us closer to the stars, and—maybe—beyond the stars, too. I will return to this later, in future workings.

My teacher has told me that one must become aware of the chakra above, in order to access the energy and use the chakra just below it. So that means I must become aware and grounded in the 8th chakra in order to use the 7th—the crown. As the 7th is spoken of as the "thousand-petaled lotus," having the use of this will certainly be mind-blowing.

Yet in my studies, I came upon a warning—if one reaches out to these chakras above the head without a firmly grounded source, one may split and become schizophrenic...two people, two viewpoints, two at odds with one another. I determine to not go any farther for awhile, simply harness what we have and build upon it a road and our own garden of desire—look at the gods and goddesses, speak with them. Studies of the third eye are in order before going beyond. For there is much to be learned.

– A Ritual Evolves –

I lay as earth while he rains down the stars of night, they are pure energies not yet grounded. As my hands go over my head to those secret chakras, I realize they are in the position of prayer, and a mudra we are all familiar with gains sufficient force over our heads.

My body becomes white, except for the red pulsing between my legs, and I create a cocoon of white silk. Within, I consume him in worship while he submits to me on his knees and drinks from me—I am his goddess. I move to the top of him and open to his seed. We share its power and grace and blaze together, circulating its energy through us

as we worship together as gods, within each other...and he speaks: "fertility, indwelling beauty, sensuality, sensitivity, receptivity, oneness, completion, energy made flesh and experiencing that flesh as our own."

He believes we have found free energy—an inexhaustible supply for the unlimited force we can turn into form. For everything and nothing are all forms of energy—everything is alive! From the gold unfolds wings, shot with rainbows, and they burn like a Phoenix...

The Prayer Mudra

Each movement we make produces a different design for our power, each design causes a different thing to happen. This is what the asanas are about. I see the importance of each. There are many to choose from. There is much to learn.

– August 3 –

He is suffering from exhaustion. This is not the time for sex with any intention. I take his head, hold it against my chest and fill him with its golden heart light. I spread it into him, and then separate it from myself by flinging my arms away, releasing him, horizontal from my body. This is energy, not more, but not less.

I will use this time to speak of method. We are using three body positions: There is the one everyone knows–the Missionary Position–this is great for lingering within our sexual chakra, igniting it, good for the end of a ritual, or its beginning.

Then, there is the Cross of Malkuth, in which our bodies are flat and straight, and our arms flung wide. The power that comes from the palms of each other can also be used as an entranceway into each other.

This avoids the urge to stay and play with that lovely sexual current we are so inclined to. The energy goes from our palms through our arms and into our heart. The sexual current stays burning in its place. You can easily rouse your burning heart on upwards, to the throat, the Ajna (third eye) chakra, and work with the powers inherent in each. One of these powers of the Ajna chakra is shapechanging. Sit up once the heart has been given fire, stretch your neck back, and stretch your arms back. They will turn into wings. The color you will see most is gold, and rainbows shifting therein. You can use this method to invoke your Holy Guardian Angel if you have the power and are safely grounded during this ritual (meaning your Manipura–your vesica smoldering, but not taking over).

Then there is–and you will see this in later rituals–what I call The Star Position. You are sitting on his lap, and you must be strong. Raise your smoldering vesica's power into your heart, filling it completely. Raise your hands above your head in a prayer. You have just reached out to the stellar chakras above the head. Subtle finger placement (only fingertips and the bottom of the hand above the wrist together) can either call that energy down into yourself–the stellar current–or you can be passive, with palms and fingers together, reaching into the current and simply leaving your hands there. They will sense powers you have not learned yet and you can become more familiar with them for future work. Although it is safe to drink the elixir of honey, the amrita that flows down into you from there, do not attempt to go into to those stellar chakras without a trained teacher.

These are the three main positions we use. Of course there are variations. Do what seems best to you. Intuition is rarely wrong.

– August 9 –

Today is the first time we have worked Nightside. What caused this? It was not our intent. I was angry with him, and it created a crack

in our atmosphere of love and trust, and through that crack the night's energy poured in...I had put the agate inside of me, as always, and that act brought it onto us.

Qulielfi emerged! For those not familiar with Her, I see Her as a spider in the center of a web, Her mouth open, filled with moon-juice. I sucked in his energy, drank it all, and I began to burn. I instructed him to take it from me, and began weaving a web around him. Again, it becomes a cocoon for him, tender in its own way, a strange protection devised for a strange world. When he came out of the darkness he tells me he is changed. Into what? I've yet to know...

– August 13 –

Different traditions have given various images to the human electro-magnetic body. Some of these are commonly agreed upon, such as the bottoms of the feet, the palms of the hand, the yoni and lingam, the "third eye." There is work to do here but today Desire clamors, "sex, sex, sex." I am close to giving in to it, when my body becomes a Lotus for him. I am passive, open, gentle. Then before me I see the Kali Yantra. Our agate eye...it erupts roots out of my body, and then into his. The eye agate becomes the Eye of his penis...the Ayin.

Our bodies begin sprouting eyes all over ourselves...!!! His lingam opens its eye and sees into me from inside. And then his entire self dissolves into me.

We are one.

Blood, breath and heart.

We have completely entered each other. He tells me he is being reborn. This must be the essence of all healing for there is no more give and take. He has taken it all, and then given it back to me in a Kiss of Light.

One.

I fill him/he fills me. I evoke the Phoenix into Us, hold our selves in

our Wings, in Love, and become part of the limitless love-ocean of all being. It's hard not to sound cliché. I say "desire is separation, union is peace," but he responds "peace is fucking me, holy..." I wonder if we are on a serotonin high.

He uses the eye agate to see inside me, and he feels hot, so hot it burns, and I cum. This gives me some relief, and I can now focus on the higher sources of energy inside us.

I sit in the lotus position, and raise my arms in the gesture of the moon...it feels as if my arms are the petals of the Lotus, and decide to call it the Lotus Gesture. Waves of pastel colors are coming off from me, and I think of all the Buddhas, sitting on their Lotuses, and wonder if there might be a hidden meaning here. My power is coming from his desire, and I put the eye agate on my third eye to see if I can raise his energy that way–it doesn't work. The agate is of earth, our eyes are Not. I remove it. My attention is on my Ajna, I become aware that I am wearing a crown.

His thoughts are elsewhere and he tells me his penis is my gateway into him...I do not use this, as I am blissing out, but will save that knowledge for later...

He raises his own attention to his heart. He has stabilized the pathway from his lingam to his heart. I have found the path to the Lotus, and it may be that he is the jewel in it.

His spirit-familiar, the black snake, writhes about me, and I am still pulsing pastels...

– August 16 –

Tonight he wants to work on the heart. Keeping down the lower fire is difficult for me...I charge my palms and hold them out to his, and we start our energy work, avoiding desire, yet using it. Transmuting it from the eye between my legs to the solar brilliance of my heart is not

an easy thing. It feels as if gravity is pushing it down—and in a way, it is. With an almost visible push, I force the fire to reach my heart. The fire below calms down to embers. Our palms are bright. I've noticed that at different times, they become different colors. This time, they resonate golden...and we join, lost in each others heart. It is beautiful, and we've decided that will be our unofficial "healing" technique.

– August 19 –

So we practice. We do not move. The golden palms, then our hearts becoming one, with eyes opened within our palms, we merged into each other's body. Our chakras brighten as they combine with each other. It gives us twice the power! This is the first time I have experienced the non-moving sadhana–I've never had the self-control, but as we work together, our abilities grow. He speaks: "I've stepped outside ego, indwelled new energies in you to interact with you...I assume energy channels I have never experienced before. I become the god. It was like an invocation of power to give to you. That was a power beyond me. The most natural energy of all."

And I wonder if it is actually a part of him that he doesn't know yet, I wonder if this is all preparation for union with eventually, everything. I am uncovering layers of his soul, and it becomes more beautiful as the layers get closer and closer to the Spark. He sees me as vast-natured, and I see him the same way...the most important thing–he found out that nature was within himself!

Here lies a danger. Our beautiful selves translate into the mundane mind like falling in love. It would be so easy to see him exalted–because I have! In my experience, I have never seen any long-term priests that continued with the same power as that which they had invoked during their rituals. But you want it, it's a desire like sexual desire. To give in, to give anything. Which is necessary during the ritual, but you MUST

take it back when the ritual is over. I am not good at this, and I suspect it won't be easy for you, either. Love hides out until the ritual series, or the relationship of priest to priestess is over. Suddenly you find yourself stuck in a muck up to your knees! Damn! What has happened? You have just "identified" him as the god outside ritual. In order to not let that happen, quick, pick another (referred to as bouncing), and let your actions prove what it is you are actually loving...!! Those around you will call you a whore, and that is exactly right! But you are a Sacred Whore.

– August 23 –

Today the unexpected happened!

My Beloved's bits were separating out from themselves, and some of the less-good bits were roaming around this time. It tried to possess me. We were both in my head. It was not his spirit, it was a Shell. Paranoia, bipolar, wild and insane. I took a shower. It didn't help. When A arrived, it was still there–waiting for sex. A suggested doing a solar invocation, because the light will disperse all shadow selves. I rang the bell, it clears the spirits. I called the Medicine Buddha, and anointed myself with the Medicine Buddha's energy, as it is solar. He was right there for me–and my aura expanded, golden and strong. A suggested destroying it, that in its roaming it could take someone else, like his younger son, who would have no defense against such a thing.

And A speaks: "The Nephesh[1] aspect of the souls unconscious/subconscious detached from the Ruach-Neschamah[2] is left in the sub-lunar worlds, semi-sentient. Solar rites are the key. The light will blast it away to its core, because it feeds on not knowing itself. It is a shadow self. It depends on the absence of light. Invoke the sun into yourself,

---

1 The uncomprehending between death and resurrection, also known as the Intermediate State.
2 The highest self, the soul.

and upon it." That is not Z My Beloved, it is the leftovers wearing his death mask. Not destroying it is like letting an undead killer on the loose. A sorcerer's shadow.

You've got to realize that the dead are not just dead. When people die there is a lot of different pieces that separate and go their way. A lot of shit goes back to the elements, and planetary and zodiacal spheres, the higher bodies stuff. But the lower self–the Nephesh, totally divorced from the Ruach-Neschamah is on the loose.

The essential numinous parts cannot be destroyed. Those parts get detached from it, it moves on, and that is the world of the angry shadows. It is a roaming disease in need of a cure. And the cure is annihilation.

So then came OUR ritual.

I put in the eye agate, and tried a pair of citrines on my breast–they didn't feel right and I took them off. Always go with what your body tells you! Later I learned that what we call citrine is actually amethyst that has been fucked with (um..heat treated).

Although we energized each other, we were both on separate trips. When we reached the heart he was suddenly gone!–he was drawing!–he had had a sudden need to draw a sigil of protection for his child, of loving him, and teaching him magicks...then he cried. And I saw him with wings, and told him so. It seems he had just drawn wings, and then given them to his child. Meanwhile, I was trying to reach my third eye...but I overshot the mark. My body became transparent, and then I saw him–My Beloved Z–the enlightened part, looking down upon me with love and concern...he was transparent as well. It appears that we all have angelic aspects–could this be our REAL Holy Guardian Angels?? Of course! I called out to him, wanting him to take me, but he will not.

Bittersweet is my love.

Bittersweet are my lovers.

– August 24 –

Sometimes a girl just wants to get laid! So I asked and we did. However, I could feel a drop in the magnetic tension between us...I fear I have abused our Purpose, whatever that might be.

– August 31 –

I speak: "All the answers are within you, and you inside me, and me inside you is the Answer."

A: "Lips a fountain of energy, I want to enter you and give you everything, explode and lose myself within you..."

I take my finger and put it into myself, draw my kala juice that is on my finger up the middle of my body, between my breasts, up my face to my third eye to my hairline, to those chakras beyond my hair. I repeat this, each time the light left behind my finger grows, over and over I trace it and as I trace it, I feel each energy center. He says, "when I feel more powerful sexual sensation in my energy body than when touching myself physically, that's how I know we are connected."

I put in the agate and he suggests making love and cuming onto it. It's a good idea but the agate will be really hard to get out from there. I no longer have periods to flush myself out.

And that brings to mind a Crone Wisdom. While we can procreate, we have the great power of creation of life. And every month we bleed and start anew. When one no longer bleeds, there is no starting anew. We simply build the power up inside ourselves...it just grows with age. A younger man, at his peak of sexuality, and an older woman, who has crone wisdom, is arguably the best combination for this work. Of course, it's not likely you will hear this from a man!

I declare myself:

"I am She, I am the Other. I am your Darkness, I am your Light. I am your refuge, I am your heart. I am around your Soul, and I hold you

within me."

I take the golden energy in my hands and run it up into the heart, stabilize that and then, with an inbreath, absorb his light. With the outbreath, I send the energy back into him along with my own.

My arms stretch out, and my body becomes a cross. His arms stretch out too–"We crucify ourselves upon each other," I say. He replies, "Golgotha and the place of ascension are one and the same. The cross of cosmic union is a mirror."

We move our light to our holy third eyes and let it fill us. Now there is a triangle of power within Us. Our hands, our chests, our Eye. "So this triangle points up..."

He replies, "There comes a point when words fail, and the actions of my body on yours speak much better of my love for the goddess you are, and who is in you, and through you. In us, from beyond our Selves. I want to taste all of you in my love."

Our ajnas touch. Mine is no longer a white glow, but has grown tentacles...they reach out to his, intertwine with his. It feels Nightside to me, and I wonder. A Nightside tree of Life, would that be a Tree of Death? And the death, what of it? Death of the ego?

Yes.

I breathe out Us, and then Us is breathed up. The back of my neck grows hot. From here, we do not need to breathe into each other. We be-come each Other.

Suddenly the power fades! I felt our energy running up my spine, up to my eye, and then out of it! It is all gone. Why? I speak to him. He is silent. No, he is unconscious, blissed out, and ASLEEP! I realize I am dependent on him for such endeavors. What we are doing can not be done alone. Damn.

– September 18 –

The night of the harvest moon, and there is lots of power floating

around out there. We connect. I flow like a river and put in the eye agate.

I speak:

"Love is an open space that lets everything in.

Love is a magnetism of Union.

Love is where we dwell together.

And you melt me away, leaving Love, the ultimate purifier."

This is all part of the ultimate surrender of the Self. This is what my priest does–he surrenders to the Goddess. This is most important to know. And one other thing–surrender is dependent on Trust. You must trust your priest.

I feel like an opening lotus, and remember that all the Buddhas sit upon a lotus flower. Is this what they are resting on? Could this be a sort of invisible way to show that formula? As I melt and flow, I take my yoni's kalas and use my index finger to draw a line of light up my body. I feel especially sweet, a lovely scent. As I draw my finger closer up my body, it becomes stronger. The trail of it glows upon my body. When my fingers meet my throat chakra, my mouth opens automatically. I stretch my neck out, catch him and pull him into my mouth. Deep blue lapis lingam..I suck him into me, self-feeding with Love as we devour each others tails as in an oribrios. Closer, closer, our astral bodies merge.

My right hand has borne the sun. My left hand bears a moon. I keep drawing my kalas up, and they become brighter and brighter upon my body. I draw my kalas to my ajna chakra, and when I reach it, I draw an eye of light there between my brows.

He sees my aura–purple and indigo, and he sees teal! Teal is the enlightened self–he is seeing my original enlightened self. That which is inside all of us. The energy of my heart rises out of my body, and into his. He does the same.

He speaks: "I am giving mine to you. You, who are the lotus in my

anima. I give you my heart. You carry it above the water to a higher sun. It is like penetrating into the higher ideal level of my inner world through a living being, you, goddess."

The more I relax into him, the lighter and brighter I feel. I can now write sigils of light, using my essence, onto my chakras. I can write images. Our bodies are blanks of parchment we can draw upon. This time, any time. And so can he. I draw Damballah over my body. He sees ourselves as Love. He says that we are "idea vehicles of individual personhood." And he surrenders in his own desire, in his essence of Self..."I want to be in you, part of you, made of you, loving you"...as he cums. But we are not done.

I draw my eye between my eyes again and again...and then I open it. It glows white and the air is cool there.

He speaks: "I cannot tell if I am in you, or you are in me. It is both. It is like we are ourselves and each other at the same time."

I continue the repeated pattern and then draw his eye on his forehead, as it merges with mine, and I cum. As I do so, he becomes my Angel! And he says, "I keep finding myself in a winged angelic female form, embracing you." I have totally enclosed him within me. I give him Her name, for he has earned it. She has accepted him into Herself.

He senses an infusion of knowledge into his heart and his third eye. "I want to come to you" he says, "kissing your heart and eyes together, to the dream of Love realized for all beings." And he calls our working, "The Interior of Purity."

– October 13 –

I prepare myself sitting in my usual asana on the bed, with my arms and hands making the fire sign before my ajna chakra. It puts me into magickal focus, opens my body's senses and brings my mind into the Now. In light and balance, I move them into the prayer position.

My priest arrives. He puts his burning palm to mine and I take it to my heart. I am charged with golden energy, and allow some of it to go into my Manipura chakra, that burning ember of continuous desire, but not letting it overwhelm me, then draw back, physically, and rend a veil with my arms, drawn back until they meet behind me. My chest is outstretched as I rend the veil, and a sweeping arc of rainbow light is left by my hands, then fades away.

I say, "I give you my body and all its secrets," and he replies, "The intent to know, and the wisdom to be Who, What and How we need to be." He is giving me the formula of his heart–the Bodhisattva Vow, present in all he does.

I kiss him. Like the palms of my hands–the eyes on them, the yoni–and its eye, the mouth too is an en-trance way into each other's bodies. And I kiss him, long, deeply, giving him the DNA sequence, the hormones, the art of passion, and the colors of love, deep inter-connectedness, self-being.

"Kissing is a language with you, that I am learning." he says.

I reply, "The tongues can also change, mutate into other forms, and can go places, unexpected places."

He surrounds us with light.

Walls melt, and we are surrounded by stars and float without gravity. I raise our arms over my head as they become rainbow wings.

I take him inside me.

We birth crowns of light. Mine has a glowing image of the syllable "om." His is red, and there is a cross with a sickle (later I learn that the night before he had done a rite with Saturn, and in his vision, his skin was peeled off there, and his skull was inscribed in gold with that sigil).

He is the King. I am the Queen. "We are angels trying to remember Who we are together...this work is a way of reminding each other through Love."

To me, this is profound.

His body merges into mine as we hold each other closely, seated inside/over him, still in asana. Our wings are around each others. "As our energies mix into each other unbound by our bodies." It is deep. We are One. I put my arms around his back and send their energy through him, and into his heart, where it radiates with mine. Our union is achieved.

All of these rituals have things in common, yet all are different, and we draw upon new techniques as we learn them. Our bodies are like stupas, the Tibetan antennae that draws down the energy of the stars and heals our planet with its force. Putting our hands into the prayer position over our heads, we reach out into the Heavens, we are drawing that stellar communion down into us. This will be of great relevance later.

– October 20 –

Throughout all we do, A keeps one objective in mind. "We are empowering each other, boosting energetic capacities and deepening perspectives. We are exploring new horizons of energetic union in the context of sacred lovemaking, intended to honor the higher powers through our innate astro-sexual energies towards the furtherance of our spiritual development. This is for the sake of all beings, and in thanks to the powers that allow us to find this."

He is basically repeating the Bodhisattva Vow. This is what keeps his motives pure. At the same time, this is also what protects us from harm, or harming.

His purpose is purer than mine. But his motivation protects us both.

He becomes like a snake, moving gently through me, and brings his 3rd eye to mine. I am soft, permeable...and I slip into him. He devours me whole, inside himself...the Goddess energy which is mine, is inside him. I am the eternal feminine inside him. Together, we are the Ouroboros,

and he says, "Our eyes merge into a new eye, and the open heart."

Yes, the open heart is essential. Without it, things surely go Nightside. Nightside magick is arguably a product of separation. Once the two become one, it changes into something much more powerful, and deeper. I believe this from the experiences I have had. All the horrors have to come out of the closet. And you find they are not horrors anymore.

We have gone beyond "sexual" now. We drift into a higher awareness, energetic shifts above are saying we are one. This moment is unity and the holiness we are framing and staring into speaks through him...

"We have become the crossroads, the cross of cosmic union and the rainbow serpent creator-creatrix intertwined about it. Our consciousness as Being, ingesting its own beingness through us in Forever. This is how beings who know Being make Love. We Are Love."

Out of trance we come, in order to have sexual love. I have become young as I pour myself into him on all levels. The coming becomes our grounding.

– October 29 –

For the first time, we are out of alignment. We have lost our path, and I am angry at him, although we have created this discord together. But I go on with our Rites. I think I've buried it inside myself. Fool.

It begins innocently enough...

I feed him in the warmth between my legs and he feels me. Our warming desire melts me and I become the Lotus under him. I hold out my arms, my palms, as golden light glows from them.

He speaks, "You are healing. You nourish me."

I see him through multiple eyes, and draw them all down into me. I feel the Nightside current within this working. I go with it, as I always do no matter what energy presents itself. No expectations = no false results. We grasp each other as the energy goes into Us. I could let

these eyes take me into him...his energy is moving into my mouth, lapis-blue—and his penis is the same color.

In the chakra system, the throat is the same blue. The syllable of this chakra is AH...my back arches, and my mouth spills out the AH as I take him inside me. He gives himself unto me. I drink him...he puts his mouth to my running river of kalas and drinks me up...I am the River of Life, and all flows into him. I am his lover—the energy flows down my mouth, neck, breasts, heart, and the eye agate tumbles out of me in the fierce current of life as I cum.

It seems that each chakra brings its own initiation, and a different sort of sexuality. –This is important to remember –.

Tranced, he says, "It is as if I have disappeared into you, and been reborn in you."

My third eye becomes the tentacled anemone. I see his golden crown upon his brow, and my tentacles go around it, into his own eye, and interlace with his own. My heart breaks open, and I thrust a star ruby into his heart. It bursts within his own and his blood becomes infected by my own.

A veve appears on my heart chakra. Its form looks like a sine wave.

At that moment, I remember seeing this before, seeing it many times over in the last few weeks. But I didn't. This is something new. I have crossed over into a shift to where it was. I have left the shift where it wasn't. I feel uneasy. This was out of alignment with our Wills. We have crossed over now, and have no way to return.

The next day he is totaled. He has been overwhelmed by the experience. This is what happens without a pure heart. This is what happens when an impurity lies within the amber light of our heart's world. He stops working with me. What have I done?

– November 1 –

It is the sacred day of Manman Brigitte, a voudoun loa considered

to be keeper of the dead. There is also a relationship between her and Hecate, though what is not clear. We decide to dedicate this ritual to her, in hopes of making it plainer. Desire rears its head, and we enter each others bodies and begin with a self-guided meditation.

We enter an underworld...there is a path through leafless trees, and I realize these are actually roots. What we are seeing with is actually a wavelength of light that we can not see with our human eyes. You can also find it inside porous bones, never exposed to daylight until death. It is a form of Ashé, the glow of Life.

We take off each other's flesh but hang them, like clothes, beside us. Our skeletons walk hand-by-hand down the path.

We tread the path and come to Her. She is pale goddess, sitting high on a pile of stones. She holds a silver cup, and into it we place our flesh. I am reminded of the caldron of Ceridwen. When we hand it back to her, it becomes water. She drinks it and light flows through her. She takes it from herself and gives it to us, in a new form. New flesh for our bones!

The light of our new forms become golden, and we hold each other. Our wings have returned, and we seem to ascend to the surface of the earth. Desire is back upon us and I pull apart my flesh to let him in. And go further. Plough me right up to my heart. As I feel my legs stretched out, my knees bent, I see our body as a manifestation of Shiva's trident.

I have talons, and I clutch him with them, drawing blood. I urge him to do the same. We drink from each other, and my body turns red. What goddess is this? I cum...

Now I extend my arms over my head in the prayer position—I am sitting upon him now, and very aware of the higher chakras above our heads. I extend my hands further, to touch the Gods...and he cums. We anoint ourselves with each other.

Even while A and I are separated, our kalas can still mix together. By that I mean that it is possible without physical proximity. If your priest

lives far from you, you can still work with him. AND you can still mix kalas! The spirit essence is not hampered by location. There is a world of men out there, and among them are priests. One may be right for you at one stage, while another may not. You may find that one serves for one part of your path, while another serves for a different one. In the words of a famous man, "Let success be your proof!"

Again, a break. I worry. I need him. I hate myself for needing anyone. But we meet a month later, and continue. Hecate beckons us on.

– December 9 –

He comes back to me. He wants to work directly with Hecate, and so we create a path with our bodies. I lay on my bed/altar.

We have two roots: our mouths are one, our lingam/yoni, another, and we fill each other with them. Everywhere else, we touch each other, and invoke Hecate into ourselves to bless us. I become the passive/magnetic lotus, and he, the electric tower to flood me with his seed. My womb is hungry. My mouth is hungry. The agate is in place...we are wet with our own juices. I draw my hand up through me, again and again. Each time, the trail of light it leaves becomes brighter. I begin making sigils all over my body with it. He sees them on his body, wherever I put my finger...he feeds the earth and the moon with us, then invokes Hecate into us as One.

She appears, "wearing" black and purple, with white skin and boney body. She is tall and her hair is long and black. She speaks: "Here is no forced purpose, the power is here to use as you wish." It is our part to see its meaning. We bleed. He takes my blood and combines it with Her's, and his own. I continue to trace the veves, the sigils, all over him... these represent the unknown energies we are invoking. They come of their own, absorbing themselves into us.

I trace them on his back as he lays over me. I trace them on his arms,

entwined around me. All of this I absorb and then release into him. Even when I don't trace them, wherever my hand passes, they appear on him. I am making a living talisman of my priest, a sacred wafer of com-union. And what might these sigils mean? They are connaissant with Her. Each sigil makes that part of his body part of her own. My mind drifts to another purification I once saw–in Java–when incensed oils were rubbed over a dancer's body, prior to him dancing a god.

Suddenly, my energy goes white!

It rises up from my heart, to my shoulders, then streams out, down my arms, and out my individual fingers, like a silken spider, I think... and then I become the spider herself. I wrap him into a bundle, not to forage for later, but as a cocoon of protection for him to metamorphize within.

It is done. In the outer world, our bodies still hunger, and so we ground them...

– December 12 –

He comes to me. I lay down on my bed/altar, naked, arms stretched out, palms open, as usual. My body is a cross for him to crucify himself on. I draw him in.

I whisper, "feel my hand. Now feel my other hand. Feel my neck near yours, and relax into me. Feel my breath on your neck. There is loving here, and a sort of peace."

He is exhausted from work, from life. I take that tension within him into me, where I can transmute it. I gently take his flesh from him, skin, muscle leaving nothing but bone. He takes mine from me. Two skeletons holding each other again. Within our bones there are many holes that serve as vessels for a part of the light that is Us. This light never sees the light of day until we are but broken bone or ash, when that certain energy is then released.

The leafless forest we stand in—no, they are roots, upside down. We are underground. We can see in this darkness because we are seeing it with different eyes, eyes that can see the colors our material ones can't. What is to others Dark, becomes our Light.

Of course, the path leads to Hecate. She is sitting on a heap of stone, and reminds me somewhat of Manman Brigitte. She holds a cup, and we put our skin into it. She mixes it and out comes new garb, skin for the wiling which we put on. These are lighter, and our wings are there. With a sudden sexual desire, we rise up, through the ground, into the sky, where the moon shines again. Our wings wrap around each other, and we enter each other entirely, as One.

And She, she is all one goddess, and she covers the entire spectrum, from the core of the earth to the stars, and then all of it becomes One within us.

– January 13, 2014 –

When he comes to me, his phallus is larger than it has been before. I find out that he has been celibate. This must, I think, be what it looks like on the astral. Men beware! I think of Austin Spare's drawings of the incubi and succubi with their great swollen members. I match him, flowing with nourishing life-giving energy and see the Kali yantra, and inside it, the Yoni symbol. And there is another inside it. Then another. They go on endlessly, an endless place for him to enter me, the sacred Feminine which I am.

Time and space have no meaning here. I create the image of an upper triangle and draw the power triangle up to my chest, creating the holy hexagram as it melds with the other. Our heart chakras glow gold, and my breasts run with kalas. One is red, the other blue, and these create another triangle, combined with my mouth. These three power points flow from me into him, and they are endless sources of

prana. I offer them to my priest. "Come and drink from me," I say. "I am as sweet as honey." I sway back and forth like a cobra. I sense the Nadi channels moving me, and a crown of white gold appears on my head as my breasts stream forth. I have become the Eternal Mother.

His secret eye, Ayin, beckons me sweetly and draws my awareness down again. Desire–all this time he is still inside me, and he dedicates his cum to Hecate. We ground together by cuming...

– January 20 –

I insert a note here for those who may not be familiar with this subject. Our bodies have a number of places of ingress. The bottoms of our feet, our palms, the eye of his phallus, the eye of my clitoris, and womb. Our mouths, our eyes, our anus. We have begun working with his Other Eye (his phallus), the Ayin, which is attributed to the Devil tarot card.

We are holding each other when I see his body of light. I want to hold him closer and increase my magnetic frequency. I give myself many arms, such as the Buddhas do, 1000 arms to clasp him closer.

I speak, "I give my self holy unto you."

A replies, "You are the sunrise dawning in my blood's fire. It is like travelling in time with you. Experiencing it from all angles, many ages of Us being held together in different moments spread across the spectrum of life. Young, old, and timeless, echoing throughout history, back and forward in dream time."

I speak, "Look with your Ayin, into me, through me, my inner body, and see the winding of the Serpent within me as it passes through the chakras. I am Eve, and I am the serpent power within me. The Devil is not what he seems. Knowledge looks like this."

My third eye (Ajna) glows brightly, another eye to open later with him. My mouth sighs, and it sighs sound like a Tibetan Ah... (ཨཱ), the

letter ascribed to the throat. Deep blue light. I feel like I have found a new secret.

I breathe him into my mouth, and give it all to him–let him absorb me, dissolving.

I speak:

You see, everything is YOU.
I contain you, you are in all of me. I am yours.
I am an extension of your sacred Being.
I am your Loving.
I am your Loving Self.
I am the Love that you ARE.
I am your Sheath. Give yourself up unto Me...

As I feel my wings behind me I raise my hands up over myself, palms meeting over my head in a mudra of Prayer. This is where the upper chakras live, those that connect to the stars.

He wishes me to consecrate something with that power. I consecrate his heat. Since he previously experienced negative effect from not grounding those energies in the past, I make a suggestion–"Let it out as colors, let them radiate off you, let them pulse out–you are a beaker filled with light."

It is important that you do not hurt your priest. Tread carefully in his magickal universe, it won't be the same as your own. Do not give him more than he can handle. When you make love, in any sort of way, you are entangling your power into his, you are energetically passing your lineage onto him. Even if you are not aware of it yourself. Such things are passed on and on...and at some time, he will pass it onto another. And as your work proceeds, he will be guided by that lineage, a Seed you have left inside him.

– February 14 –

Stoking the forces within, it has been some time and we are both hungry for each other. He sees all of our energy centers turning into eyes. The eyes kiss, and then merge, and we become one giant angelic Being.

We are the Beginning, and our colors are like that of an opal, or an interstellar cloud. Soft, pulsing, merging like sperm and egg, we co-create. More, we ARE CREATION. We are timeless or perhaps time moves so slowly we can't feel it. Our egos can separate and watch Us through a mirror of the mind. That is the Watcher, which is always within us.

This fusion is the essence of Love.

Being a Babalon is Being Love.

Now we are going to begin our studies on the Sahasvara, the 7th chakra and the one above. According to my research, in order to gain control over the chakra below it, one must have the experience of contacting the one above it. In gaining awareness of the 8th chakra, we should be able to master lucid dreaming, past lives, and what we learn from them. This is new territory for us and the quest is on.

He comes to me naked and filled with his holy intention within me and through me. We become One inside each other–our chakras become one, and correspondingly, they double in intensity.

We lay inside one another in the act of Holy Creation.

He speaks, "This creation is always there, with or without us. It encompasses all."

And it feels like the only thing that is REAL.

He drips sperm into me slowly, as is natural for men, some more, some less. He is more...continuous...he is a fountain of the divine seeds of life. My hands and arms multiply endlessly, and his does as well. These are in multiple dimensions, and they are all holding each other–

endlessly–outside Time–we are holding onto each other.

Our combined selves make our fluids combine too, into the Elixir of Life, golden honey it appears as, dripping down into Us. It burns into our flesh–my yoni, his Ayin, at the tip of his penis. He can use it to see right into me, up the center of my being. It travels like a snake. It is the kundalini and it winds up through me, reaches my head, and stops at my 3rd eye.

I take the middle finger of my right hand, and begin at my vagina, my eye, trailing the elixir, the honey path, up to my Ajna eye. I repeat this over and over, and it becomes deeper, deep into my flesh, and brighter...yes, brighter with each pass.

I open my third eye and absorb it all into me.

He speaks, "All of me is rushing into you, awakening in you as an extension of me. We are alike."

He feels the presence of the Divine Feminine within himself.

Now we begin our journey up...the honey of the Ajna transmits itself into a clearer, more golden, potent honey, purer than we had sensed before, almost transparent. I can feel it beginning to drip down upon us.

I raise my arms above my head, in a praying position, like an arrow, pointing upwards towards the eventual goal. My hands are now inside the 8th chakra, drawing its connection to me, I realize it is there from where the honey drips down upon us. My hand position changes. My index and middle fingers meet my thumbs. My energy meets itself at that point, reminding me of the Tibetan vajra. The place where those six digits meet contains a brilliant spark of light. Then my hands spread open and out, creating the sign of the Vessica over me. In the space between them–inside that Vessica, I see a horned crescent moon of light, as if it is hanging in the stars over me. I find that if I want to stop this process, I can return to the vajra position and maintain that bright Light.

I realize that I have 3 portals open: the Yoni, the Ajna, and my mudra Vessica.

With my mouth, I blow out this living stellar current into him, a light blue breath. It goes into his mouth, his lungs. I fill his lungs as he fills me.

We exist within that timeless sacred space in a universe of our own making...

He tells me that the Light has changed him. It has changed me, too.

He speaks, "This Work is beyond duality. Both sexes are a part of a higher cosmic androgyny. Our Being is beyond sexual. We just have knowledge of the poles from the experience in union of cosmic manifestation."

I respond, "Yes, beyond duality but still re-incarnating into it as one or the other, just as we reincarnate into different selves, different situations. It is said that touching the 8th chakra also opens the experience of that Unity."

Throughout this, he has not physically cum. We do so then, grounding ourselves back to the earth.

– March 21, Spring Equinox –

We've accidently run into each other. "Time to celebrate spring!" I think. But that is not what happens. The life-affirming energy of sun and flowers have broken winter's grip. There is a sense of wholeness about me, as well as holiness in the occasion of our union. But this rite was not to be what I imagined it as.

I sigh deeply as I connect with him...with that outward breath, I empty my Self and then breathe him into me. We pulse at-one-ment together. With each breath I breathe out, the incoming breath brings more of him into me until I am wholy-filled by him. We become one and the channel is complete.

He is working with Hecate now, and so I call upon Her current.

I say, "You become the Answer to all my Questions. You are a deep darkness that is in every part of me...ah! Sweet darkness!"

He responds, "Your darkness." And he calls upon his goddess.

My hair suddenly becomes a mass of writhing snakes about my head. They all open their mouths, desiring him, and reach out to him. They want to initiate him with their Touch.

He answers, "I want them, each and every one."

I speak, "Come, and tell me what you see, in my dark cavern."

He speaks, "I see bat-like wings on my back, and I become a dragon. Inside you, fire and a bright sun-like flame."

I respond, "Take it as you take the serpents." His Ayin appears to my eyes in vision before me. I orgasm, but it does not stay near my yoni. Instead it goes right up my spine and into and above my head in shades of bright blue-white energy. It changes and I see golden light, preserved in space, and realize this is a kala–the Alchemical Gold, that we have created in our union. He offers it up.

And that becomes our Rite of Spring.

Not having a goal–a set purpose–within our rites can be a helpful thing. You do not get pre-conditioned responses. If you know nothing, and something happens, you can look afterwards and see how your visions and energy-work relate to the record you are reading afterwards. The negative of this is, of course, that you are not prepared. You have to trust your body not to undertake that which you are not ready for.

There are times when such workings become dangerous to the rest of the body–and to our priests, too. Within the chakras that are located in the body, one can always go to the heart, become that golden glow and chase off any darkness you have come upon, and become your Holy Guardian Angel! We hold a lot of power inside our bodies but we never know its full extent until we awaken it with another.

During comm-union, we give it back to our priests, who can choose either to send it back, manifested fully, and then we can render it up a notch, a higher octave. This is a way we work together, to mirror our own sources and extend them farther than we believe it possible. All the energy points of the body are involved. We have our chakras, our hair, our auric energy, magnetism/electrical energy to work with. Both yours and theirs. Each chakra contains within it a new type of initiation. Each is unexpected. The movement from one to the other clears out the others before it. They are relatively safe to work with.

We all come from a mix of traditions here. Our vision can encompass them all, or a part of them–that which you or he feels closest to. Hence comes the mixed symbolism that runs throughout my practices. Imprints are made in our auras–we see the sigils, yantras, and images there. They empower our rites, or become gateways to enter into.

We all come from a mix of ages, as well. Some of us have ceased our bleeding. This is no deterrent. When we stop bleeding, our energies build up–there is no monthly cleaning out. This, then, can be a most significant time to work. This is the time of the Crone. It is said that the crone has many types of knowledge, and this is why. A Crone can be most knowledgeable in terms of her past experience, and also, can contain the most power.

By now, we have learned how to transform ourselves into anything we desire (shapechanging). We can recognize potential priests by the feeling of familiarity–the existence of the archetypes within. We have learned where our "points of entry" are (yoni, lingam, mouth, anus, and the Ajna) in our/their bodies.

– July 1 –

He opens his aura and heart to me and I slowly and softly blow prana into him. This stellar light streams down from above our heads,

passes through our third eyes, into our mouths. (This can be practiced alone, as a breathe meditation, as well. It is very important to draw upon the free energy around you, so that you do not deplete your own.)

The stuff of life fills his body, as he collects it within the central channel at his back.

"What do you see?" I ask.

He replies, "I went through a flame in my heart and beheld myself there as if in a mirror as the Angel, fiery and colorful. Realized that those were my eyes, the fire is myself in the heart, that the heart is as the ego and the angel as well."

I raise my arms over our heads, and make the prayer mudra. My hands are, essentially, in the chakra above our crowns, within the chakra that is over us. We are praying to Each Other–all of them–and drops of the sacred Dew, an octave higher than the kalas below us, drip down and into our physical bodies.

"Someday you will find that you are Love. And you will find that that is the free energy around Us. And you will find that pain is, in essence, anything that takes you away or blocks you from that Self. The pulse of you is in your crown and that energy comes down into your Ajna eye."

"Together," he says, "they are the New Cognition."

He practices breathing through his palms, like Reiki energy, sent outwards to fuel the flame, grow a seed, and connects it to his heart, the seat of the Soul.

In Tibetan Buddhism, the heart is regarded as the seat of the soul.

A: "I see through illusion, through phenomena, to the numinous."

He is, essentially, clearing the path, so that others can follow. This is the point, the unselfish motivation that keeps us here. This is altruistic motivation. This is what sanctifies such work as our own.

"It feels like it's coming back to me, like someone else waking up inside the head I've been trapped in until now. Look at the spirit within

me, press your eye and heart into mine, look at Spirit as a flame in a desert becoming a Tree of Life. My soul is capable of entering you and feeling all you feel as my own, We are one."

But I am greedy and want it all. I express a desire for our Angels to merge, and he responds, "We are on that bridge. Open the eyes! The flame and the spirit are One. Now give this love, give it back to the source."

"I only want you." say I.

"I don't exist," he replies, and–I realize–HE'S GOT IT!

"This is the Love that worlds are born from. I want to see this seed as the gods see it. That is my prayer. To know what they know, the holy eternal seed of fire and spirit."

"But your life is your Tree, and your heart is your Seed." I respond.

"Cum with me in thanks and request to be pure enough to see as the Gods do, this holy thing."

And so we cum together. It takes forever, and is but a moment of time. "This is a new way to pray. Proof we can tune this to the right channel, the higher frequency." he says.

It is now that I wonder–have we accomplished what we were meant to do? For there are many more chakras to explore. We have only worked with those inside and next to our physical bodies. There is the 8th chakra, and the 9th, 10th, 11th, 12th...a new vision invites us on, into the knowledge and conversation with the universe, within the multiverse. Shall we go on? In Tibetan Buddhism, the deity is imaged on the top of one's head...the stellar rays reach into the image, causing it to come to life. You drain that deity into your body, into your heart. It is the safest way to work with them. The sweet amrita rains down upon you. You and your priest take its blessings.

Going into them is quite a different story. Another story for another time in another body.

Blessings to all of you. May you find joy in this work. The time of the rising of the female power is at hand. ✣

Babalon by Dianne Mystérieux

"Watch Her Wrap Her Legs Around this World": Babalon, Sex, Death, Conception, Punk Rock and the Mysteries

by Lou Hotchkiss Knives

I. Chanson de la plus haute Tour

> It was not Death, for I stood up,
> And all the Dead, lie down –
> It was not Night, for all the Bells
> Put out their Tongues, for Noon.
> –Emily Dickinson

It could be one of those codeine dreams, as it is so vivid I can make out every fibre in the carpet, every stain on the floorboards, with incredible detail. But it isn't. This dream is something else.

I'm sitting with my daughter by a window in a spartan, shabby top-floor flat. The place looks strange, with retro furniture, this could be the 1930s, maybe the 50s, it's hard to tell. My daughter is the age she would be now had she lived, almost two years old. It's early autumn and it's raining hard. We are sitting on a worn

carpet looking at the city below.

The spectacle that offers itself to us is truly apocalyptic. The sky is low, with black clouds rolling over the distant skyscrapers, their Babel-like silver silhouettes gleaming like moonlight on a blade as they are hit by hundreds of raging thunderbolts. Electrical cables rupture and dance for a second in the twilight like maddened snakes, spitting furious sparkles, before disappearing in the relentless, stroboscopic, Bosh-like Inferno that engulfs the scene.

I do not know what this place is, nor why we are here. But I know we are pilgrims, a shivering pair of wanderers, a dreamtime witch mother and her ever-silent moonchild, marooned by oniric tides in the middle of this monstrous city of steel, glass and concrete; a city where no one ever seems to dare wandering outdoors, so terrifying is the thunderstorm outside.

There is a tower in the centre of the city, where the storm dwells at its most violent. It is higher than the others, and from my outlook, it seems at the mercy of the wrath of the elements more than any other building.

This is where we're going. This is where She dwells.

Anxiously, we make our way through the flooded, deserted streets. I notice I'm carrying a red umbrella trimmed with black lace, a sure sign that She is watching over us, somehow. I am fully aware of the danger of undertaking this journey, but I know She wants us to come to Her, so we bravely soldier on.

In the twinkling of an eye, the scenery changes again, and we find ourselves at the top of the Tower, by what looks like a penthouse flat surrounded by a patio. We have arrived. Here we are, in the holy of holies, in the very heart of the storm. The scene is terrifying, unfathomable. Lines of pure electricity surround us, crackling menacingly, forming a web of perfect geometrical proportions around the place. Lightning bolts hit

the structure every couple of seconds, and thunder shakes the ground under our feet. I dare not move, or touch anything, for fear of electrocution. I'm growing increasingly uneasy. I glance at my daughter. As usual, she stands nearby, silent, her eyes serious, her little face impassive.

Where the hell am I?...

The feeling of dread stupefies me.

Then I see Her.

She looks a bit like Lisbeth Salander at the end of the movie *The Girl with a Dragon Tattoo*, at the moment when, having finally defeated the patriarchal foe, the heroine emerges gracefully out of a car into her new life *incognito* in Southern France, her appearance radically transformed by plastic surgery. She is stunning. She's wearing an elegant taupe taylor suit, and her pale copper hair falls impeccably on her slender shoulders.

But at that moment, it is not Her beauty that transfixes me. It is her eyes. Standing in the doorway of the building, she is basking in the violence of the elements, embracing the scene with her pale grey gaze, a gaze which all at once radiates murderous bliss, sexual abandon, and the tender promise of the impending, catastrophic cataclysm.

She is pure Destruction.

I know there will be no mercy, not for me, not for anyone. She is the End of the World made flesh, the Omega, wanton devastation. I want to flee, this is too much, too intense, but I can't move. The air is thick with energy, heavy with annihilation. She barely looks at me. *This is it,* she seems to say without a word. *Thou art not glad thou meddled with magick? There is no other way, dear fool, it is the eleventh hour.*

I wake up in my bed, feeling disturbed. The oppression of the scene I've just left still lingers in my mouth. In the grey light of dawn, the

wind-swept trees outside seem almost tranquil after the Biblical wrath of Babalon's storm. My daughter is gone. *Of course she's gone.*

It is only later, as I consign my oniric journey in my magickal diary, that the penny drops and the significance of the experience hits me, and I am filled with gratefulness for the understanding she has bestowed upon me.

On the ruby brick road to Babalon, I have travelled in many guises. I have donned the priestess' robes, the garter of the courtesan, worn the heavy boots of the punk activist, and flaunted the insolent pagan nakedness of the lover, of the mistress. Babalon has been my initiatrix, my guide, a demanding teacher on the path towards the understanding and the perfection of my own womanhood, of my own Witchcraft.

Many a time I had walked on the edge of her Abyss, peering in awe into the depths, careful to maintain my balance and remain on the straight and narrow. Gladly I had embraced the challenges and acknowledged the dangers inherent to her devotion, with Hubbard's warning to Parsons in Liber 49 always on my mind:

"She is flame of life, power of darkness, she destroys with a glance, she may take thy soul. She feeds upon the death of men... Beautiful... Horrible."

I'm having a breakthrough. I realize that I had never fully grasped the meaning of these words until this moment. I repeat the passage to myself as the Knowledge sinks in, embedding itself in my soul. *"Beautiful... Horrible."* I think of Semele, one of Zeus' many adulterous fancies, who burst into flames after making the mistake of asking her divine lover to show himself to her in his true form. Mortals aren't generally built to stand the sight of Divine Splendour. Hell, now I can totally understand why. *She may take thy soul...* Too right.

"Beautiful... Horrible..."

There was Babalon. Destruction as the unavoidable, ugly twin mask of Love. There she stood, offering me a glimpse of an uncomfortable,

yet certain future: the doom of a civilization drunk on profit, whose industrial excesses are slowly but surely sowing the seeds of the tragedies of tomorrow. The drought, the storm, the flood, the hunger, the Cataclysm ahead, and through it, the vision of my own annihilation.

Fuck me, that was scary.

I know there is no point trying to hide and pretend it's not already happening. She is an apocalyptic goddess, and as her devotee I am aware I must embrace that side of her. In fact, if I'm being honest, I know I was long overdue a little reality-check.

I'm glad for the lesson. So glad. *I love you,* I blurt out, looking up as if expecting to see her face in the pale morning sky. My heart swells in awe of Her.

I become aware of Her Cycle of Manifestation.

Destruction. Death. La Petite Mort, Orgasm. Sex. Flesh. Love. Life.
The urgency of Life. Destruction again.

II. In Utero

Babes alone in Babalon
Out of the Storm, out of the Storm
      –Husbands N Knives

Born–Bridalled–
Shrouded–
In a Day
Tri-Victory–
      –Emily Dickinson

Babylon means "Gateway of the Gods" and such is the lesson of the Scarlet Woman, Babalon, the Mother of Harlots and the Abominations

of the Earth. The Mystery that dwells within us is that our bodies are gates between the Worlds. Through sex we connect with the primeval powers of Life and Death, cloaking in flesh, in physical matter the naked souls of the Unborn.

My daughter first called me from beyond the Veil in June 2011. *I'm coming, I'm coming,* her soul was screaming with child-like joy as it was crossing the ether like a comet, as it was haunting my meditations with the warning of her imminent arrival. *You'll be pregnant with me by Lugnasadh.*

Shock. Horror. I shuddered her voice away, disturbed. Me, pregnant? No way. I wasn't even trying. I wasn't going to. Hell, I *hated* kids.

My journey through womanhood had been a bumpy one. After two years of emotional and physical abuse as a child at the hands of other teenagers, I had been left with plenty of bottled up anger and feelings of deep inadequacy around my own femininity. After years of healing, soul searching, and relentless magickal exploration, Babalon came into my life and gradually mended what had been broken. Tenderly, she put the chalice to my lips, and pushed the sword in my hand. She crowned me with roses and stood me naked before her mirror. With a kiss she demanded I let go of the shame, the sorrow, the hatred and embrace myself as she embraced me. She commanded that I cast away the old, false garment of oppression to be reborn in Her, for the Love of Her, her exhortation echoing that of John Dee and Edward Kelley's Daughter of Fortitude:

> *Purge your streets, O ye sons of men, and wash your houses clean; make yourselves holy, and put on righteousness. Cast out your old strumpets, and burn their clothes; abstain from the company of other women that are defiled, that are sluttish, and not so handsome and beautiful as I, and then will I come and dwell amongst you: and behold, I will bring forth children*

unto you, and they shall be the Sons of Comfort. I will open my garments, and stand naked before you, that your love may be more enflamed toward me.

And it was. I woke up one Sunday morning feeling that a huge weight had irremediably been lifted from my shoulders, that I had been given a clean slate of sorts, and that I was about to embark on the magickal journey of my Life.

I remember the exact moment the Word became Flesh and my daughter finally landed from her Tiphareth into my Malkuth. It was shortly before Lughnasadh, just as she had predicted. I hadn't been trying. I was still in denial.

The Mystery, though, was unfolding inside of me. The mystery of the hungry cunt devouring cock, gorging on desire, and that, through the union of Yoni and Lingham ignites the spark of Life, and clothes pure Love with flesh. The Matrix spins the wheel of physical existence into motion. Yet, in effect, the soul's dwelling within the flesh is only temporary. We only pass through the Gateway of the womb, into Life, only to go out again, at the time of our Death, through the Gateway of the tomb, that mirror matrix where matter decays and only ashes remain. As such, the womb is the first initiation on the path to the storm-torn Tower, where Babalon awaits in all her destructive, eschatological glory, guarding the liminal space that separates this life from the next.

I've only ever seen my daughter's face in the no-man's land of my dream journeys to Babalon. She dwells in the oniric Babylon that lies beneath the realm of Sleep, waiting for me, a silent, loving guide on my journey. I lost my pregnancy early, birthing a pitiful mess, the tragic, derisory pieces of a broken Cupid, the blood relics of a beautiful, passionate, meaningful, larger-than-life love. Such is the dance of Babalon, *Beautiful... Horrible.* Awe-inspiring and implacable, yet

glorious and magnificent. In the end, all that we are must be poured into Her cup, filled with the blood of Saints and the wine of our fornications. We will dissolve back in Pure Love. We shall crumble to dust and be reborn.

In the East, Tantrikas on the left-hand path are encouraged to spend time in graveyards, amongst the partly cremated, rotting remnants of human beings of all castes, and the incessant Kali-led ballet of scavenging dogs and carrions. The place is favourable to meditation upon the impermanence of things, or to indulge in taboo breaking, such as copulation amongst dead bodies, as to surrender one's sense of abhorrence as sacrifice. The adept must rise to see in his lover, the initiatrix, the face of Kali, the Destroyer, at the moment he makes love to her as Shakti. If we are, as Babalon devotees, to become the agents of the Storm she unleashes upon the World, and embody the avatar Jack Parsons called "The Woman Girt with the Sword," we must not shy away from knowing her wholly as both Lover and Destroyer. We are the Witchcraft, and all witchcraft dwells in the body of Woman.

I have kept the remains of my child, tucked to sleep with a small cuddly toy in a red box filled with dried rose petals. It rests on my altar, a reminder of my initiation, a talisman, a precious relic. The Secret is that nothing is ever lost. All is transformed. It is one of the primeval laws of physics, as it is of existence. Let us remember that the XVIth arcana of the tarot, the Tower, is followed in sequence order by that of the Star. Divine enlightenment, renewal, the calm after the Storm.

Through the experiences of love, sex, conception (be it physical, artistic or metaphorical) and death, we come closer to the Mysteries of womanhood, which are the mysteries of Babalon.

La Petite Mort, Orgasm. Sex. Flesh. Love. Life. The urgency of Life. Destruction. Death. Conception...

III. Kabbalistic notions of Union/Conception and Death/Rebirth

Conception: a word which originates from the medieval French "concepcion," meaning to grasp, to comprehend. In the liminal world of Womb and Tomb, the act of conception is therefore one of manifest understanding.

Let us now embark on a little cosmic exploration trip, so as to apprehend these concepts of Union, Conception, Birth and Destruction and how they relate to Babalon on a whole different level. On the Tree of Life, the three horizontal paths that run across the Pillars will prove particularly important to our study. If you are new to Kabbalah, you may find some of the concepts presented here a bit obscure, so you may fast forward to the next bit if you wish. Alternatively, if you are curious, bear with us, arm yourself with patience and get prepared for a lot of reading, cross-referencing and pondering. The results will be worth it.

A. Daleth: The Door

Let us start at the top of the Tree with the path that links the Mother Goddess sphere of Binah (Understanding, realization) and the masculine Chokmah (Wisdom, the power of Creation, energy). It is associated with the letter Daleth, the Door. Here, the Door is understood as womb, as *gateway to the Gods*. It won't come as a surprise to you that the tarot card attributed to this path is that of the Empress, giving us a supernal vision of Babalon as a triumphant Nature goddess who clothes the soul in matter, gives form to energy, and brings forth existence from the upper realms of non-existence. If you look at the Tarot trump on the Rider-Waite tarot, you may be excused to think

that the Empress figure represented here is indeed pregnant. Have a look. What do you think? Bump or no bump? The question has divided occultists for at least a hundred years, but ultimately, regardless of the answer, you cannot deny that the meaning of this card is about conception and birth. The Empress is also associated with Venus, in the Roman sense: a goddess of Nature as well as Sex. On a more abstract level, the Daleth path is the path of artists, as the balance of wisdom and understanding is necessary to channel and create works of Beauty.

The concepts expressed in Daleth, of Creation through Balance and Union, manifest again at several other levels of the Tree of Life, as we're about to explore.

Daleth runs parallel to two other paths which also mirror and emphasize this idea. So let us continue our journey. From Binah, the abode of Babalon on the pillar of Severity, let us travel diagonally, down across the Abyss, to reach the sphere of Chesed, on the pillar of Mercy.

B. Tet: The Serpent

Here begins the first of these two paths. Situated below the Abyss, it is known as Tet, "the Serpent." It connects Geburah (Severity, the Will) to Chesed (Mercy, Unconditional Love). Tet is associated with the tarot card of Strength, number VIII, in the Rider-Waite tarot. On this Arcana we are shown the image of a woman gently submitting a lion. This imagery is reminiscent of the union of Babalon and the Beast, so the trump was naturally renamed Lust in Aleister Crowley's Thoth Tarot, and beautifully illustrated by a depiction of our lady Babalon lasciviously riding the Beast. But the two cards take a slightly different angle on the Woman's relationship to the Beast: The Strength tarot trump offers the vision of a tender, but sexless, submission of the Lion. This is an allegory for the willing, loving submission of the ego/animal nature to the Higher Self. This is about lovingly surrendering to our true Will.

By contrast, Atu XI, Lust (note how the numbers have changed, Crowley having quietly attributed the number VIII to Adjustment, or Justice, instead) shows a more raunchy depiction of the same principle. Here, Tet is a path that celebrates sexual union, and the sacred marriage of Babalon and Beast. Because the path is situated just below the abyss, the conception which takes place here is that of a new Self. Note that Lust, trump number XI in the Thoth/Crowley tarot, is therefore placed directly under Daath, the eleventh Sphere, providing a key to understanding the card's meaning. Take the components of 11, 1 and 1, you have 2, hinting at the creation formula 2=0.

"For I am divided for Love's sake, for the chance of union."
— AL 1:29

What makes this trump really interesting, once you start looking into the symbolism of it, is that it raises a lot of questions as to the exact archetypal function of each protagonist. Who's who exactly, in this union of Whore and Beast? Is Babalon representing the feminine Love of Chesed, or, as the one who owns the reins, is she the Will of Geburah incarnate? Is the Red Beast representing the violent aspect of the 5th sephiroth, or, being the ridden one on the picture, does he represent the Love that lies under the Will, the latter symbolized by the female rider? The answer is probably a bit of both. If you are a familiar lover of Babalon, you'll probably have noticed this, whilst lost in her embrace: the boundaries between ride and rider are always blurred. You ride and yet you're being ridden. You each partake of the essence of the other.

To me, the challenge offered by Tet, also known as *The Path of the Daughter of the Flaming Sword*, is to finally surrender the ego, dissolving it into the cup of Babalon so that the marriage of the higher self with the ego/animal nature is complete. This path is there to

prepare the adept for the challenge of the Abyss. By letting go of the ego, abandoning dated concepts of who he thought he was (or she was), by dissolving, drowning his whole being into Her Chalice, the magician offers him/herself willingly in a loving sacrifice to Babalon.

The Chalice is therefore a key to understanding this trump. It is, like Daleth, a *door* towards rebirth, a matrix filled with potential for regeneration. It is also filled with sexual nectar, *the wine of her fornications,* and reminds us that Babalon stands for life, laughter and divine drunkenness. Yet, because it must be filled by the blood of the adept, the chalice also stands for the sacrificial cup, a place where the energies of Life and Death mingle. This message is as much about the Will to Die than it is about the Will of Life.

This path of marriage, of Union, of dissolution by Hieros Gamos which the coupling of Babalon and the Beast illustrates, has been attributed, as we've seen, to the Hebrew letter Tet, the Serpent. This is an allusion to kundalini, as this quote from Liber Al Legis suggests:

> *"I am the Secret Serpent coiled about to spring: in my coiling there is joy. If I lift up my head, I and my Nuit are one. If I droop down my head, and shoot forth venom, then is rapture of the earth, and I and the earth are one."*
>
> – AL 2:26

You don't need to be Ronald Hutton to get that this is about sex and tantric magick. "If I lift up my head..." may refer to the supernal vision of the path just above, Daleth, the Door, of which we've already talked about. "If I droop down my head, and shoot forth venom, then is rapture of the earth"... This could be a reference to the next parallel path, that which lies closer to Malkuth and the Earth. So let us travel down one level and examine this third and final horizontal path.

C. Peh: The Mouth

Linking the spheres of Hod (the intellect, the mind, communications) and Netzach (our instincts and emotions), it is called Peh, "the Mouth" (another conceptual aperture, like "the Door" of Daleth). Here we find an evocative vision of Babalon the Destroyer. Surprise surprise, the Tarot card associated with Peh is... Yep, the Tower. A tower not unlike that of my dream: storm-torn and ravaged by lightening, it symbolically reminds us that to achieve balance between our intellect and instincts, comfortable but false beliefs and behaviour patterns must be destroyed. Extreme stances must be abandoned. Like the Tower of Babel–this bordello of linguistic confusion and emotional turmoil–once fell, so must our inner tower, so we can liberate ourselves from anything that prevents us from understanding our true identity as spiritual beings. The challenge of Peh mirrors thus, on a personality level, that of Tet on the soul level. Something in us must die, and we must embrace that change. Once the Tower has fallen and balance has been restored, the symbol of the Mouth, associated with this path, begins to make sense: with the intellect (Hod) and the intuition (Netzach) speaking with one voice, the Word becomes a vector for eternal truths. We're not going to pretend the Mouth isn't a sexual organ, either. Just like the Door/womb of Daleth and the Cup of Babalon of Tet, the Mouth brings us back to that liminal, primeval space where the Great Mysteries are enacted and 0=2.

D. The Middle Pillar

There is more, dear readers. When we incarnate, we travel down the Middle Pillar from Kether to Malkuth to be born on this earthly plane, in the World of Assiah... But notice how, when we travel up the same pillar towards Kether again, we encounter first a rather phallic

Tower as the path crosses that of Peh, then the cosmic union of Babalon and Beast at the next intersection, that of Tet; to finally be confronted with the vision of the pregnant Empress on the path of Daleth.

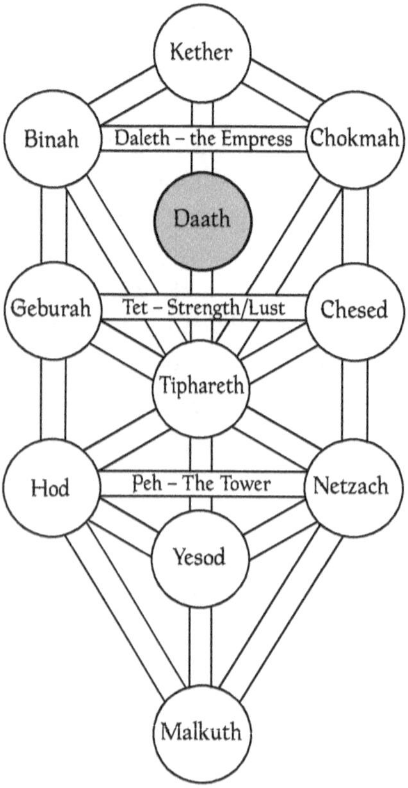

The three horizontal Kabbalistic Paths

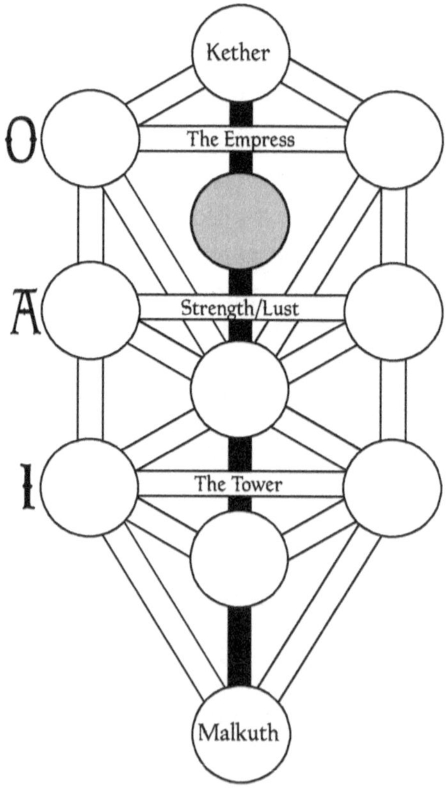

The three paths in relation to the IAO formula.

Stretching ourselves a little, we could imagine that each parallel path could be associated with one of the letters of the magickal formula IAO: the erection of I for Peh, the lasciviously open legs of A for Tet, and the enclosed, womb-like O of Daleth. From this angle, IAO would

signify the generative union of the masculine and feminine principles. But this time, the incarnation (de-incarnation?) takes place in reverse, from Malkuth to Kether. What could be the lesson for us here? That when the physical body dies, and the soul travels back towards pure spirit, it undergoes another kind of reverse conception and rebirth, this time *ad-nihilo?* I shall leave you to ponder where this journey leads, and how it fits with your personal understanding of the Tree of Life... In the meantime, let us go back to the nitty-gritty.

> Flesh. Love. Life. The urgency of Life. Destruction. Death.
> *La Petite Mort,* Orgasm. Sex. Flesh.

It is now time for us to resume Babalon's rose-strewn pilgrimage. After the Flesh, the womb, after the Tree, let us look at Conception on mind level, on artistic terms. Artistic creation is another way to manifest the Mysteries. Those of you who paint, sculpt, write, rhyme, or play music will no doubt agree: the spiritual and the artistic are easy bed fellows. Through art we inevitably touch on those eternal concepts of sex, conception, and destruction. Punk rock, with its occult dalliances and hedonistic values, makes no exception to the rule.

IV. Sex Pistols: And the Word became Flesh, and Stage-Dived Amongst Us

We stand on stage at Plymouth Punx picnic 2012. It's midnight–the witching hour–and my band, Husbands N Knives, is finally about to start playing after hours of waiting. The venue is full of exhilarated rock enthusiasts, and the smell of sweat and stale beer permeates throughout the room. From his raised booth, the sound guy raises his thumb, a signal that all is ready to roll. We glance at each other, briefly nod in acknowledgement, like a bunch of paratroopers about to jump from a plane. From my bandmate Julie's guitar, the first notes of "Rage" rip into the silence, immediately followed by the furious roll of

the drums. To our delight, the song, an ode to Witchcraft and female rebellion through the ages, immediately sets the crowd into motion. A group of lanky, spiked haired girls start to mosh, soon joined by an Asian boy in a black lace dress and New Rock boots. The ones who have been there all day, drinking cider in the sun, muster the strength to nod their head in rhythm. The old punks gather by the stage, clutching their drinks, their dishevelled silhouettes surreal against the multicoloured lights of the projectors. Their support and energy galvanise us as the tidal wave of music reaches a crescendo.

> *"And from apple to snake, from the gallows to the stake*
> *I am the Gaping Hole, the Terror of Church and State...*
> *Rage, Woman is Rage, Woman is Rage..."*

As I sing those lines, I remember the years spent furiously scribbling lyrics in the solitude of my room, an angry young woman determined to set the world on fire with punchlines as vitriolic as Molotov cocktails. As far as I can remember, I have always yearned to be a performer and a songwriter. I have always written short stories, poems, lyrics and in many ways writing has been my salvation. I have written songs to kill the pain, to give an outlet to my frustrations. I have written songs to mock the world, put the comedy back in Life and take the sting away from Existence. Punk Farce. Catharsis. Then I discovered Magick and the whole endeavour took a whole new twist. Combining writing and performing with Witchcraft in such an energy-raising context as punk rock is an incredibly powerful and transforming experience.

Punk rock, as an artistic and cultural current, has Babalon smeared all over it. The word punk, for a start, first appears around the times of King Charles II of England, in the late 17th century. After years of austere puritan rule under Oliver Cromwell, the coronation of Charles II marked the beginning of an era where dancing, drunkenness,

shameless adultery and licentious literature flourished like never before. We all remember Nell Gwyn, the whore-turned-actress-turned-royal mistress, whose scrumptious beauty and savage wits came to embody the spirit of that period. Nell Gwyn was, in Restoration terms, a true *punk,* and by this we're not referring to her very working-class sense of humour. In 17th century vernacular, a punk was a prostitute. If, later on, the word came to describe a young male ruffian or gangster, let us not forget that the Holy Whore had a claim to it from day one.

Punk exudes sex and rebelliousness. From Nina Hagen masturbating on German television to Nancy Spungen's opiate-fuelled romance, from Vice Squad and its leather-attired singer Becki Bondage, all the way to a lipstick-smeared and lingerie clad Courtney Love roaring "I was a teenage whore" on the first single of her band, the aptly named Hole, punk history is full of Babalon-type females whose antics have transformed and continue to shape the face of Rock n Roll. More than any other musical current before, punk allowed women to smash the slick, polite, politically correct carcans that had restricted female artistic expression up until the late 20th century. Whilst a doe-eyed Stevie Nicks had sweetly sung about witches, the likes of the Slits and L7 had taken upon themselves to act like ones, screeching at the top of their voices like raging succubi, shamelessly intoxicated and popping boys' (and girls') cherries faster than they could pop pills. The *beautiful/ horrible* dichotomy that Hubbard refers to in the Book of Babalon finds its full expression and embodiment in their art. Through punk rock women allowed themselves to be in turn sirens and harpies, sublime and grotesque, endearing and revolting, conquering and wounded, sexy and cheap. Through their art they challenged the conservatism of western values, took a stand for women's rights and challenged the sexism of a male-dominated music industry. Like the conspiring witches of old at their secret sabbaths, they gathered during the 1990s in Riot Grrrl chapters dotted around the world, sang and drank, fell in

love with each other and plotted a revolution. Their anger is far from showing signs of abating. In the early 2010s, Russian feminist band Pussy Riot sent shockwaves across the planet by openly defying the Russian Orthodox Church with their Punk Prayer. Don't tell me punk rock is dead, or that it's given up on changing the world.

> *"For within you is the song that will shatter the silence, the flame that will burn away the dross."*
> – Jack Parsons, *The Woman Girt With the Sword*

The Path of a Witch with a foot on the punk rock scene is, as expected, not exempt of dangers, and shadows lurk in every corner. Working with Babalon through the medium of songwriting and performing is exhilarating, but make no mistake, it's not all a bed of roses (sorry to break the news, Jon Bon Jovi). Occultist or wannabe rock-star, the pitfalls are often the same. Drugs are an obvious first. Aleister Crowley was as strung out as Kurt Cobain was. You take heroin, for inspiration or gnosis, and one day you stop taking it. It takes you, and the Great Beast 666 was the first one to admit it. Should you choose to use them, drugs can be a means, but when they start becoming an end, you know you're in trouble.

Believing in your own hype is another common trap.

> *"One of the great dangers inherent within the practice of Magic, and all the occult arts–is the development of an enormous egotism characterized by messianic feelings, infantile omnipotence and the destruction of any capacity for effective self-criticism."*
> – Israel Regardie, *The Complete Golden Dawn System of Magic*

My, that reads just like a description of Axl Rose. But again, it is easy to slip down that slippery slope, whether we write songs, conduct rituals or both. Musick is Magick, as Oryelle Defesnestrate-Bascule

puts it, pointing out that both words vibrate to the gematria value of 156, Babalon's sacred number. To continue channeling songs from above, a musician must remember to put the ego on hold and listen to the music of the spheres. The mouth becomes the womb that births songs born from the waves of the Great Sea. And it doesn't matter if your song sounds like nails scratching a blackboard. Babalon lingers in jarring verse and perfect melody alike. Those of you who have listened to Babes in Toyland and Queen Adreena will back me up on that. What's really important is your intent and the purity of our offering. It's all about the DIY approach. Let go of your expectations, let the spirit take shape in between your lips. Let her speak through you. Music is therapy, self-discovery, a magical tool for pushing boundaries and finding who we really are.

Like Womanhood, like Magick, music comes with its own set of initiations. Years ago I was told the story of one such initiation by a beautiful and talented shaman of a folk musician, a former member of 1990s pagan protest band Heathens All. For years and years, Tina had had a recurrent nightmare she was struggling to make sense of. In the dream, she was flying around in space, a disincarnate spirit, only to find her progress blocked by what she described as a wall of discordant, cacophonic noise which was so unbearable that she would inevitably, at that point, wake up in a jolt. One day, as she found herself sharing her dream experience with a group of friends, someone suggested that, next time she'd find herself faced with the wall of sound, she should try to go through it and put it behind her. So she did... What happened next she described as a turning point in her life. As her spirit took the challenge and penetrated the wall, she found the once unbearable discordance turning into the most beautiful harmony she had ever heard. Her soul glided upwards effortlessly, blissful, elated by the wonderful music that seemed to emanate from the very fabric of the Universe. That morning, she awoke with the calm, strange certitude

that something in her had slotted back into place. Out of the blue, she started feeling compelled to learn music and write songs. Had she discovered her True Will?... Twenty years or so later, Tina Bridgeman still entrances audiences with the poignant beauty of her inspired, heart-felt folk tunes.

> "Write, & find ecstasy in writing! Work, & be our bed in working! Thrill with the joy of life & death! Ah! thy death shall be lovely: whoso seeth it shall be glad. Thy death shall be the seal of the promise of our agelong love. Come! lift up thine heart & rejoice! We are one; we are none."
> – Aleister Crowley, *Liber Al Legis* 2:66

Magickal artistic conception can take interesting twists when you write music as part of a band. As the only practicing occultist in Husbands N Knives, I had not expected that the creative spiritual energy I was channeling would somehow start manifesting through my band mates.

Playing music as a band can be a devotional act. On a creative and ritual level, one interpretation of the basic punk band setup (vocals, guitar, bass and drums) is that each instrument stands for a magical quarter or element. The drums stand for Earth and the Body. Drums are amongst the oldest instruments known. The World's first drums were made of wood, clay, animal parts, all earthy materials. The first, primeval drumbeat is of course that of the heart; on a macrocosmic level, it is the rhythm of the universe, forever expanding and contracting. When you drum with a drumkit, your full body is engaged; in this regard drum practice is akin to dancing. The drums, by connecting their player to the primeval, tribal beat of our ancestors, earth the song into the ground.

The Guitar, which, as we'll see, is sacred to Babalon, naturally

partakes of her fiery energy and passion. Both phallic and feminine in shape, it exudes aggression and sleaze. Its music, along with the vocals, determines the melodic upper layer of the song. On the other hand, the bass guitar's melody, like water, flows in between the sonic energies of guitar and drums. If drums stand for earth and bones, the bass stands for the pumping blood, and the rhythm of the tides. The bass may be shaped like the guitar, but its pitch and vibration is lower and closer to that of the drums. Bass and Drums make up the rhythm section of the band, their partnership of Water and Earth setting the base of the primeval "EarthBeat" celebrated by the Slits in their 1981 eponymous song.

The bass's melodic function is to bridge the fire of the guitar's tune with the drum's earthy rhythm. Vocals, of course, convey the energy of Air: communications, the intellect, the power of words. Singing technique draws on visualization and breath control: singing practice can therefore be a form of meditation. Melissa Cross, in the *Zen of Screaming*, explores what she calls "unclean" vocal techniques by offering a range of exercises that turn screaming and growling into a true discipline.

The Spirit comes alive in the music created by the four musical elements working together. When all members are aware of their instrument's symbolic function, they can channel the qualities of their given elemental and jamming can then become a ritual.

I am sure many musicians amongst you will have experienced first hand how prophetic and psychic song writing can be, especially when it is a joined effort.

The journey into Punk and magick took up from there. With the Whore as our Muse, songs came to us in dreams, or during ritual. At gigs, feedbacks in the sound system sometimes seemed to take a life of their own, gracing our most occult numbers with new harmonies that sounded almost as if someone else was playing alongside us onstage. In

the studio, strange happenings spooked our producer, as an invisible presence insisted on playing havoc with the recordings, erasing certain lyrics which quoted the Book of Babalon mid-sentence, forcing us to record them again and again, seven, eight times... *Her sacred number, and that of the Babylonian Innanna.* After photoshoots, we'd find ourselves looking at photographs where the smoke in the room had taken the shape of dragons and strange beasts floating around us.

Not that all of this wasn't expected, somehow. After all, isn't Rock N Roll mythology full of urban tales of musicians selling their soul to the Devil, occult incantations in records played backwards, and spellbound Catholic schoolgirls throwing their wet knickers at cute guitar heroes?

Recent studies have suggested that the distorted sounds emitted by electric guitars trigger in the human mind an evolutionary response: as the sounds resemble the cries of fear and effort of combat or hunting situations, we respond to them with adrenaline rushes and delicious frissons, not too dissimilar to the ones we get when watching horror films. In *The Spiritual Guitar Guide,* published in 2003, David Cherubim, an occultist and musician based in Los Angeles, explores the link between guitar playing and magickal practice. The first form of the guitar dating back to Ancient Babylonia, the instrument, inevitably, finds itself placed under the aegid of the Holy Whore. For Cherubim, its modern shape, reminiscent of the female body, places it under the direct rule of Binah, the Kabbalistic sphere which is home to Babalon. In its electric form, the guitar also becomes the instrument of Lucifer, the Flaming Sword, the wand of the magician, the light bringer, the weapon with which to fight the war of the Holy Whore. Its twenty-two frets (not counting the open fret) are reminiscent of the twenty-two major Arcana of the Tarot, and of course of the twenty-two paths that run along the Tree of Life. Guitar playing, he argues, is a discipline akin to yoga and martial arts. Mindful chord and scale practice become a meditation where the boundaries between musician and instrument

dissolve and union manifests in Music.

The Red Hot Chili Peppers said it best: rock music is all about Blood, Sugar, Sex, and Magick.

> Sex. Flesh. Love. Life. The urgency of Life. Destruction. Death. *La Petite Mort*, Orgasm. Sex...

V. THE WIFE – WITHOUT THE SIGN

> *Kiss to kiss, breath to breath,*
> *My soul surrenders astonished to death*
> — Patti Smith, *Frederick*

> *When you ride, you're ridden*
> — Marilyn Manson, *Misery Machine*

So now has come the time to go back to the root of it all. Love. Sex.

We get a glimpse of the sexual Mysteries of Babalon if we ponder the significance of her sacred attributes: the Sword and the Chalice. On one hand, Babalon is predatory, sexually and spiritually assertive; the reins in her hand on the Lust Tarot card symbolize the firm control she exerts over her consort the Beast. As a Lover, she in an initiatrix who challenges man to meet her in bed as an equal. She seduces All and embraces All, and as such the expressions of her love, desire and arousal are central to her identity. The sword, which is sacred to her, is the weapon of the conquering sex warrior, of the woman who, fully embracing her power, stays true to her own desires and freely picks her mate amongst equals. Its corresponding organ is the clitoris, the most phallic-like of our female organs, the little war-like Bouddicca which presides over the logistics of sexual pleasure.

> *Woman, put up unworthy weapons. Put up malice and poison, false frigidity and false stupidity. Draw the sword, the two-edged sword*

of freedom, and call for a man to meet you in fair combat, a man fit for your husband, fit father for your eagle brood.

– Jack Parsons

On the other hand, Babalon also embodies the receptive, womb-like qualities of the Chalice which she holds. The Whore's sex is open to All, as the 12th Aethyr stipulates:

This is the Mystery of Babylon, the Mother of Abominations, and this is the mystery of her adulteries, for she hath yielded up herself to everything that liveth, and hath become a partaker in its mystery. And because she hath made her self the servant of each, therefore is she become the mistress of all. Not as yet canst thou comprehend her glory.

These two aspects are complementary. Babalon is sexually assertive, conquering; yet she is also all-accepting, unrapable in her all-encompassing desire. Because of this, sexuality is one area where women working with Babalon can end up facing a complex challenge.

A. Standing in the way of the Sword

We live in a world that both worships and loathes Babalon. Centuries of Christian hegemony have left us with a lingering disdain for the flesh, the love of which the Neo-Platonists regarded as an inferior expression of divine Love. Woman's unbridled sexuality is still considered a threat to the foundations of society: attempts by religious groups to restrict young women's access to contraception and sexual health centers, for instance, are testament to this. They fear such facilities would render teens "promiscuous" and therefore steer them away from the acceptable framework of monogamy, marriage and maternity. The debate over prostitution is shunned by political authorities, whilst stereotypes and conflicting opinions around the

role of the sex worker within the community abound. Portrayals of sex workers in the media tend to swing between the extremes: the affluent, glamourous Belle de Jour on one hand, and the trafficked, crack-fuelled victim of gang violence on the other. The truth is that the experience of prostitution is extremely varied and depends on many factors. The current political stance of beating around the bush, for questions of morality, or for fear of acknowledging the real economic power held by sex in our societies, has important consequences. Not only does it prevent the (majorly) female workforce from benefitting from the social advantages of exercising a recognized profession (such as pensions), but it also prevents the guarantee of better work conditions. Prostitutes offer an intimate service which has the potential of bringing genuine enrichment to both parties on a human level. Sex as an experience can be healing, relaxing, comforting, exhilarating, releasing. Should sex work be more highly regarded, it could exert a truly positive role across society as a whole. In the past, Sacred Prostitution offered the promise of religious experience through the sexual encounter of the pilgrim and the priestess. The latter were regarded as holding a valued social role.

Broadly speaking, in the capitalist world, sexual freedom in women is encouraged as long as it feeds the fantasies of the patriarchy. Social attitudes to sexually liberated females in the West are ambivalent: their freedom and ease with their own bodies fascinate, yet threaten and repulse. Porn stars and pin-ups are celebrated, but heavens forbid they should be educated as well as sexy. This would be too much to handle. Sex sirens must be trivialized as to not appear too threatening. They should inspire sexual desire, but not Love, and certainly not both, for then their power would be absolute. Men in the 80s weren't encouraged by the tabloids to write lyrical love sonnets to Samantha Fox, although some probably did. The female body is not publicly worshipped in the spiritual sense of the word, it is commodified, rated, leered at in an attempt to negate its power. Street slang has all kinds

of charming nicknames for female genitals, the sacred yoni of yore: *beef curtains, bloody axewound, kebab, hairy Mary*. These attitudes stem as well, of course, from our own insecurities. As Peter Grey argues in his excellent work on Babalon, *The Red Goddess,* the vision of Beauty and desirability can arouse fears of rejection and feelings of inadequacies in both men and women: confronting Babalon the Bombshell is to confront the ego. It is only natural to want to be loved, to be accepted; deep down most of us are scared of abandonment and betrayal. The Beauty industry feeds on these anxieties like a vampire *in* a blood bank. Socially, too many young women struggle in the atmosphere of constant fear and competition that body image issues generate. This *Ugly Sister Syndrome* manifests in jealousy, depression, constant comparisons with others, body-worries, and the incapacity to appreciate and embrace our unique beauty. As Grey points out, part of our Babalon work will involve addressing those fears and work at transcending them, so the Goddess can truly express herself through us and our bodies.

B. Standing in the Way of the Chalice

If accepting and embodying the Conquering, sword-wielding Babalon in ourselves and others can be a challenge, becoming the receptive, Chalice-like, All-accepting Whore in our sexual magickal practice can prove equally problematic.

Sexual assault and rape are experiences that at least a quarter of the female population will experience at some stage in their lives. The fear of rape is drilled into us from a very young age, and as we grow up, stories of date-rape, drug-rape and domestic abuse reinforce the feeling of unease and the fear that, should we fully embrace our desires, femininity and sexuality, we would expose ourselves to violence, coercion, pain, degradation or worse. Victim-blaming attitudes, conscious or

not, are still rife: if a girl gets drunk, she shouldn't complain if she is raped; sexy outfits send the message that you're asking for it, and in some cases, an uncovered head or bare legs can be enough to have you branded a filthy slut. Let us not pretend that these attitudes are anything new: the history of Babalon is marred with repression and violence. How many women, because of the fear of rape, cannot fully open during sex, even to a loving partner?

This fear of rape results in a fear of letting go, a fear of penetration, a fear of our own desires; worse, it perpetuates ignorance around our own bodies and their mechanisms. How many young women still wait for a man to make them climax, rather than take control of their own pleasure? Although the market for sex toys is gradually addressing the situation, sex education still shies away from tackling the complexity of female pleasure.

If we are to fully embody Babalon during sex, we need to confront our uneasiness and liberate ourselves from the shackles of our fears. The magazine *Psychology Today*, in an article published in December 2010, estimates that 25 to 40% of women will admit to having had rape fantasies at least once. Fantasies like that are not easily shared in public, especially as many of us have been, at one point in our lives or another, confronted by the reality of sexual violence; besides, the argument that women secretly enjoy rape is commonly used by abusers to justify and seek to excuse their crimes. Where do such fantasies stem from? In her book *King Kong Theory*, punk feminist writer Virginie Despentes argues that they are a hang-up from Christian doctrines that celebrate women as ever-suffering, willing martyrs. She recalls the morbid erotic fascination that Sunday-school depictions of female saints, bound and tortured, had had upon her as a child. As a rape survivor herself, Despentes believes that these fantasies are the expression of a deeply-engrained cultural scheme which encourages women to take a sort of masochistic pleasure in their own victimization. Better cum against

your will, we are told, and surrender to male superiority, relishing in their absolute power over you, than meet your partner as an equal and cum willingly like some dirty Jezebel. In this context, women are not allowed desires or choices. The only freedom left to them is to embrace their own oppression, *no no no,* rather than *yes yes yes,* is the accepted line.

This argument aside, why else are we, indeed, having those fantasies? Partly because they enable us to reclaim control over our fears by turning them into pleasant erotic thoughts. Partly because, for some of us, such fantasies allow us to get around some unconscious lingering guilt over our desires: if someone else is doing it to us, then it's all OK, we can cling to the pretence that we're "good girls" in the Sunday-school sense.

Although Despentes makes a valid point, I have a slightly different angle of interpretation. For a start, the term "rape fantasy" isn't really accurate. When we fantasise, we are not helpless victims, rather we actually are the only ones in control. We are the ones who imagine the scene, picture the protagonists, decide on their actions and take pleasure in our musings. No one is taking advantage of us, rather, we allow ourselves to become the unrapable, and embody the all-receiving Chalice. No matter how violent our fantasy, in the scenarios we make up, we are, in truth, always willing, forever enacting the archetype of the Whore who gleefully takes it. A real-life rape situation would in effect deprive us of this absolute control, which is why the argument that women enjoy being forced just doesn't hold.

In a cultural context which values penetration over reception, and which encourages, as Starhawk puts it, *power-over* rather than *power-with,* freedom can be found by turning paradigms on their heads and re-appropriating our own pleasure.

How many of us live in bondage to our fears? Or, as Jack Parsons puts it, in his essay *The Woman Girt With the Sword:*

"How long have you served in chains, a slave to the lust of pigs and the guilt of pigs?"

The practice of sexual bondage offers one way to face our demons and transcend our taboos. Through bondage we get to re-enact our most intimate fantasies, but with a partner, which means complete trust will be a *sine qua non*. Decisions about the use of safe words, and personal boundaries, will allow trust and intimacy to flourish, whilst allowing you to let go sexually. Everyone wins: the partner who isn't bound will develop a more precise reading of his/her lover's body and reactions, paying attention to subtle movements and energy changes, and intimacy will be reinforced. With their physical jerks constrained by gag and rope, the bound partner will reach new states of awareness and become more focused on physical sensations. This is where the experience of truly opening begins. Physical restraint allows only for limited control over one's movements, forcing one to relinquish their fears and fully trust their partner. Gradually, you will be able to truly become the Chalice, opening your body, mind and spirit to the experience, and reaching a place where fear and pain get transcended and higher states are attained. Thus will you be able to truly embody Babalon.

C. Hieros Gamos

On your journeys of exploration of the sexual potential of Babalon, you may well be tempted to ask Her to send a partner your way with whom to study the Mysteries. Be aware that as a Goddess of Love and War, She may well decide to broaden your experience of Love by placing on your path lovers who will challenge you. Don't go there expecting it to be easy. Don't expect a straight A* privately-educated Disney Prince with his eye on marriage. Goddesses of Love tend to have a particular sense of humour, so brace yourself for one potential hell of

a ride. The priest may well turn out to be your best male friend, your neighbour's husband or wife, or your boss. Expect the transgressive and the unexpected. Be prepared to explore uncharted territory. If you are not prepared to push the boundaries, break personal taboos, or to suffer for Love, then you will not truly understand its full power.

Work at your relationship, make it beautiful, make it devotional. Craft it. Learn from it. Your love is another path to Her.

> *"And thou who thinkest to seek Her, know thy seeking and yearning shall avail thee not unless thou knowest the mystery; that if that which thou seekest thou findest not within thee, then thou wilt never find it without thee. For behold, She has been with thee from the beginning; and She is that which is attained at the end of desire."*
> – Doreen Valiente, *The Charge of the Goddess.*

You may become her bride someday. Maybe you have already. She has many lovers.

Have you ever made love to her? Let me tell you this, with a smile and a wink of complicity: she's the best ride in the Universe. You'll see. I'll be the storyteller, I'll set the scene for you. Let us go on one final journey. I've kept the best bit for the end. Tonight you are the Whore, and she has chosen you.

The candles give a golden glow and her incense billows in the room, filling your lungs with rose, jasmine, storax, the sensuous fragrances of whoredom. You are wearing the mask, the garter, the sword and nothing else. As you invoke her, a shower of stars shimmers behind your mind's eye, and there she is. Babalon descends upon you like a pornographic re-enactment of the Visitation of the Virgin Mary, setting your senses on fire. Her energy envelops you in an imperious caress. You may be taken aback a little. If you are new upon the path,

chances are you didn't initiate this. Always the teacher, she tends to pop your spiritual cherry only when the time is right. You don't have much time to ask questions. Your whole being, to the very core of your soul, suddenly contracts around your root chakra, like a coil tightening in gleeful anticipation of sexual release. At the base of your spine, the dual serpent of kundalini awakes and stirs. You feel light-headed, overwhelmed with desire. *Open me up, fuck me, set me free,* screams your soul in the silence of the ritual room, a willing sacrifice, as Emily Dickinson puts it, to *Calvaries of Love*.

You lie down as she appears to you in flashes behind your closed eyelids, crowned with the Moon and the Sun, astonishingly perfect in her beautiful nakedness. You drink the sight of every part of her body with hungry reverence. Your love radiates towards her and softly, your energies meet and start dissolving into one another's, revolving in a loop that dances from cunt to mouth and mouth to cunt. The Serpent rises a little more with each sweet pang of pleasure. Your blood is pumping symphonies of divine ecstasy. You're getting off on each other. You've hit the place where hearts meet in the knowledge that they are one, made of the same pure divine Love, when lovers gaze into each other's eyes and know they are looking at themselves. And still the flow carries on, relentless, mouth to cunt, cunt to mouth. *Whose mouth, whose cunt?* The boundaries are so blurred that you are not sure when she begins and you end anymore, or who rides who. *When you ride, you're ridden.*

You hit the point of Union as your entire being dissolves into hers. The Serpent reaches the crown chakra, energy exploding out of the top of your head only to rush back into the root and up again. Here is divine ecstasy, revelation, recognition, transformation through Union.

"I love you! I yearn to you! Pale or purple, veiled or voluptuous, I who am all pleasure and purple and drunkenness of the innermost

sense, desire you. Put on the wings, and arouse the coiled splendour within you: come unto me! To me! Sing the rapturous love songs unto me! Burn to me perfume! Drink to me, for I love you! I love you! I am the blue lidded daughter of sunset, I am the naked brilliance of the voluptuous night sky. To me! To me!"

– Gnostic Mass

Orgasm. Sex. Flesh. Love. Life. The urgency of Life. Destruction. Death. *La Petite Mort...* Orgasm... The Circle is complete, yet the dance never ends.

You've spilt the blood, annihilated the ego. Radiant, She floods the World with Life and Beauty.
She dwells within you. You are a banner before armies.

My Love is a Pandora's box of Sorrows. My Love is the rose-strewn calvary, the cilice for the soul, the bloodied pilgrimage of Babalon. My Love is a shirt of nettles, broken black diamonds over my pillow, the clawed foot of Lilith Kilili, the shining brow of Samael.

My Love is the Whore at Her window, the gold coin on her lap, the acceptance of one and all, Filth and Gold, Roses in the Gutter.
My Love is Sappho leaping, the lavish Roman luxury of Her torture chamber, the space between the stars, the suffering of Saints.

My Love is a moth to a snapdragon, my face buried in my lover's hair, a night to hide from the woes of the World, a kiss falling from the heavens like a snowflake, the Union of the Mystic and the Rose. My Love is the Holy Song of desire and need, words for Wyrd, carefully crafted verses, music for the End of Days, sweet nothings whispered in Paradise.

My Love has eyes filled with fire and brimstone. My Love is Hope raging in a Box. My Love crowned me with Roses and the Thorns have dug deep into my face, a holocaust of Ruby, tears of Blood as tokens to her Utmost Glory.

In Nomine Babalon
– Beltane 2014

REFERENCES AND SUGGESTED READING

Babalon, Thelema: Aleister Crowley, *Liber Al Legis*.

Drugs: Aleister Crowley, *Diary of a Drug Fiend;* Julian Vayne, *Pharmakon: Drugs and the Imagination*.

Music: David Cherubim, *The Spiritual Guitar Guide*.

Sex, Feminism, Prostitution, Pornography, Punk rock: Virginie Despentes, *King Kong Theory*.

Kaballah, the Tarot: Naomi Ozianec, *The Kaballah Experience*.

Babalon, the Politics of the Aeon: John Whitesides Parsons, *Three Essays of Freedom*.

Babalon: Peter Grey, *The Red Goddess*.

Sex and Politics: Starhawk, *Dreaming the Dark: Sex, Magick, and Politics*.

Untitled by Ayahna Kumarroy

Sex and Possession / Voodoo Love
The Gede We Always Knew Was There

by Lilith Dorsey

I can't talk about sex without talking about love. It's very hard and very easy to write about love. In a way I think there is nothing else to write about. It is life, it is a little death, it is the divine circumstance where one equals two, and vice versa. Haitian Vodou and New Orleans Voodoo both have a pantheon of Loa/Lwa, or deities, that survive and thrive on love and sexual passion. There are the Marassa beyond traditional male and female on the corporeal level, a cosmic union of polarities. There is Damballa and Aida Wedo, the sacred serpent and the rainbow that has now become the stuff of legend.

If there is an equivalent to Babalon it would be Erzulie, also known as Ezili, who is love dramatically personified. There are as many different avatars for her as there are faces of love. There is Erzulie Freda Dahomey who is said to weep an ocean full of tears because people fail to keep their promises. There is the fiery Erzulie Taureau, who mounts everyone like a bull to show her dominant prowess. Erzulie Dantor is the strong protector of abused women, who fights with all she has to defend those that need her assistance. There are the Barons and the Gede, they are the lustiest bastards out there, watch out is what I have to say about that for now.

Normally, in my experience sex and possession are not a usual part of New Orleans Voodoo or Haitian Vodou. There is a custom of spirit marriage among certain spiritual houses in Haiti. This is not entered into lightly and it is treated in many ways like a genuine marriage. In some instances even a marriage license is obtained, a ceremony is performed and the betrothed then spends a period of time wed to the Lwa/Loa. This can be a single day, a week, or for an entire year and sometimes even a separate sleeping location in the house is secured. Sometimes this is done to prove to the Lwa/Loa that the individual is ready to be married to a human individual. My understanding is that this does not involve possession, or actual sex either, but rather more a time for dedication and honoring.

Most often in the traditions of New Orleans Voodoo and Haitian Vodou sex is kept separate from spiritual practices. Altars and shrines are located separate from the bedroom, sometimes even in a separate building. I usually explain this to newcomers to the tradition by asking them if they would have sex in front of their grandparents or the Queen of England, usually their answer is no. Unlike with Babalon, it is not respectful for sex to take place in front of these energies, despite the orgiastic ritual Voodoo frenzy that Hollywood movies frequently depict. There is nothing inherently prudish in these beliefs, it is just thought that the two behaviors do not go together.

Possession is a hotbed topic of late, it seems like every Neo-Pagan tradition is ready to employ trance possession as part of their practices. I have no issue with this if it is executed thoughtfully and responsibly. I have been involved in dozens of ceremonies involving possession mainly within the afro-diasporan context, but also those of other traditions. Possession is a true mystery. It's one of those aspects of Voodoo that strikes fear in the hearts of men. I think because at its core it's about control. The whole process seems to scare people, when it should inspire them. I've spoken a lot about what Voodoo sacred

possession isn't. It isn't slapping a goddess in the face, it isn't vomiting pea soup, it probably isn't what you think it is.

As with union with Babalon, possession, like good sex is a divine coupling. A union where both parties benefit, and become more than they were before. It is unlikely anyone's first time with sex or possession will go smoothly.

And you shall see the shades which she becomes
by Madeleine Ledespencer

The Warrior Babalon

by Maegdlyn Morris

Babalon is not perfect, she cannot be. She has experienced the full spectrum of human bliss, suffering, ecstasy and sorrow. She is not subject to the whims of a man, she councils rulers and watches over the sex workers all while swirling and rampaging through the muse aspect for her countless lovers and artists. She moves through the creative world inspiring memes on the web, and rabble-rousing tribes to build an ever bigger bonfire! Babalon feeds the sick and offers healing to the broken spirit but only when they seek to heal themselves. She removes boundaries and guilt, and destroys the sexual doubt and shadows that society uses to control. All of this she does without concern for socially imposed taboos. As a result she is reviled, called a bitch, a slut, a whore, and all of these she welcomes and channels into power. She may offer her body at the slightest invitation to those who have desire, without any expectation of love or respect, because it suits her needs and her will. Her power comes from serving her True Will and NO ONE ELSE!

Society does not often welcome this vision of feminine power. The woman that questions authority and places her own desire above that of current legal or moral standards and norms is a serious threat indeed. What happens when a community that has found itself tied to the fifty hour work week for low wages and terrible conditions begins to find itself questioning authority, brought on by the wild

tempestuous relationship of a Scarlet Woman? The current paradigm of social control depends on the ignorance and willful sleep of the masses. If they become inspired with sex, art, creativity, and freedom, all hell can break loose! Laws must be passed and sermons must be preached, to keep her from completely destroying the dominant social structure. Babalon encourages self awakening, even though it can include chaos and a breakdown of what we thought we knew. She provides the inspiration, the strength and the "I dare you to step out of line" that has been the beginning of many an artists' careers.

As I put further thought into my personal understanding of Babalon I am reminded of the temporary natures of our bodies. We are so much more than the bag of skin we currently inhabit. Flesh is only a vessel to hold the universe's image of itself and, as we age, if we are lucky we learn to recognize this aspect of self.

The festival universe often represents Babalon in her original form; young, powerful, filled with beauty and passion. This is one of her strongest and most popular aspects. Yet there are so many more faces that she wears! I had a conversation with Nema (Horus Maat Lodge) about this topic. She gave a workshop where she said simply, "What happens when Babalon gets old?" As a culture, Thelema has thrived and expanded through several generations of family. We have female youth moving into the current as well as our elders who are transitioning through the veil. All of these women have something to offer the movement. Knowledge, wisdom and experience come at many ages, not just the age of youth and fertility.

How does the Scarlet Woman manifest in modern culture? She is seen in the female politician that sells herself in order to gain the power necessary to change the world. She is the single mother in West Virginia dancing happily on table tops to earn a solid wage. She is the musician that cuts off her hair so the audience hears her words before her Beauty. She is the young girl that learns to create her own

weapons and hunt her own food despite what her peers might think. Babalon is the aging woman who still loves heavy metal and LSD. She can be found in every corner of the world. The Black Widows of Chechnya that opt to blow up a military checkpoint that murdered their village, the root woman that helps her tribe maintain population control, the widow that runs for public office in a world of burkas. All these aspects represent the energy that is Babalon. She is the key to the future of true freedoms from the tyranny of public thought. Seek her out and she will reward you with endless opportunities for bliss, passion and chaos. This is not a ride for the faint of heart, some do not want to be woken up, and are perfectly content to live their entire lives confined within the illusory chains of dogma, but for those willing to risk a wild adventure, Babalon makes herself available, freely and without restraint.

When examining the many faces of Babalon, it is easy to glorify the kind, receptive, youthful flame. My personal experience has been of a darker nature, perhaps undertaken through the side gate, the dream world of forgotten magick and long years spent dwelling in the Tree of Life sphere of Malkuth. Babalon represents all aspects of the sexual current. Hers is not to judge your nature nor to apply the human invention of guilt. Babalon is also free of the notion that sex is for procreation. While children are sometimes a welcome and joyful side effect of the sexual encounter, the human mammal is designed to enjoy sex all of the time not just while in heat.

So then, from a magical perspective what are some of the ways in which the sexual current has been used to connect with the divine current that is Babalon? I explored Sado-masochism as a way to make money, and seek entrance into the astral through dark doorways as a young woman and it met all of my expectations and more. I quickly realized that like other experiences of an extreme nature S&M was highly addictive, and that if not given the highest respect would

ultimately devour my ability to enjoy other more subtle forms of erotic pleasure. I treat it as any other volatile form of consciousness altering; it is dangerous and thus highly effective.

This is about my experience, no one else. I write from within. It was critical in my experimentations that I be able to separate the erotic aspect from the adrenaline aspect when I first began to experiment. My first teacher was an unattractive older man with erectile dysfunction, who repulsed me in an erotic sense. He was highly skilled with weapons and tools of torture so when I approached him, it was with the understanding that he would teach me the ropes, so to speak, without the complication of romance. I quickly found that I was able to use fear as an excellent method for what I called astral travel. When he told me to trust him and then he set my chest on fire the thrill was incredible. I was compelled to place my being utterly and completely within his control.

Then as fast as this had occurred he placed a whip in my hand and commanded me to cause pain to someone else. The psychic whiplash was intoxicating and heady; I was drawn into this gray world of magick, philosophy, ethics, emotional baggage, the roller coaster of pure fear followed by screaming bliss, wrapped up in one tight package. The sense of power, trust and control that is brought through extreme play is one that I acknowledged and took as my own. Today I can quickly move inside of someone's comfort zone, find their soft spot, massage it, make it scream with an appeal for mercy, let it rest then move it back up into a frenzy of desire, that forgets to hold boundaries. This state is one that I carry within me all the time and I show it only to the extreme few that are capable of handling the results.

The Babalon that wields a whip or bows to one is easily misunderstood. The secret to power exchange is not necessarily that of pain or fear, although these are delicious tools. The power that she brings is that of stepping outside the boundaries of acceptable behavior

and demanding more. She reaches down inside the willing Beast and rips out his vulnerability, expands it to the size of his entire universe, sets it on fire and then dances around it watching as it burns. She holds the Beast in her arms as he weeps and reveals his inner-most shadows, and they celebrate the sense of release as his sparks light up the sky, or in some cases burn the house to the ground. The art of playing with the senses is one that hopefully I will never completely master, as the journey is the best part of the voyage.

Edge play in the S&M community is called such because the participants are experimenting with boundaries, pushing beyond them, testing the edges of their control, pain thresholds, emotional endurance and so on. While this in and of itself is exhilarating, for Babalon, edge play is something much more. It is the rare individual that is enough in touch with her self that she can allow someone else to attempt to tear that self away. Babalon uses the principles of edge play to introduce her magician to life without ego, without the mask, with the ultimate goal of being able to plunge into the Abyss free of expectation or goals. Once her magician has reached this space, Babalon waits for them and receives their experiences, satisfied in the knowledge that she as been a witness to ego death and willful change.

This is a power that can be held by Babalon at any age and experience gives her the tools to continue opening the gates for those with the courage to pass through them. She cannot be owned, controlled or defiled because she belongs only to herself. Her lovers are secret, there is nothing to be gained by being seen as her consort for she is the spiritual consort of all, providing the passage to self-knowledge to those who know how to ask. To claim kinship is to lose her because she will not be owned, nor claimed by any person.

Her true consort is the one capable of accepting her in the Twilight, under the black moon when the full power of lust, passion and severity is awake and swirling about happily, without shying away, without

criticism. She values their judgement above all else because they are the ones that can truly see her. In this world between worlds when they makes themselves known, she will give of herself freely and completely welcoming the spectrum of dark fantasies, and rewarding their gift with her flesh. It is not necessary for her lovers to be an earthly vision of lust. Babalon is capable of seeing the potential in all lovers capable of seeing her. They may be old, young, disabled, deranged, filthy or clean. None of this matters except for their ability to hold space and accept without question the flames of her lust. The Babalon of whom I speak may offend some. I am a heretic. I have taken no formal training and my visions come from within. I make no claims of dogmatic knowledge.

There are many types of Babalons, however, I speak of the Babalon of Severity, of Geburah. This Babalon is not to be tested for she will seek to destroy the ego. She will take delight in wrecking the fragile mirage that protects the Ignorant. Be careful when you approach her because she will cause change to occur and it will not be comfortable. When you come across Babalon dancing for money, worship her respectfully and honor her with coin of the realm, for she holds many forms and all of them are worthy. Babalon will also reside in retirement for as time passes she will age and become wise and wrinkled. This aspect of the Crone has a bountiful gift for those balanced and sensitive enough to receive it. She has a lifetime of crashing through boundaries, leaping off the cliffs of socially imposed behavior, and thriving above it all. She is still a sexual being who has the capacity to share great secrets when approached with the reverence she has earned.

The Babalon of Severity is a confidant to rulers, lover of politicians, Scarlet Woman to magicians. One of her most powerful attributes is the ability to keep confidences, to protect her consort to the grave when necessary. Sometimes this means that she cannot mourn, cannot openly claim the grief that is hers, instead suffering in solitude. This is the cost of her discretion and one of her most powerful tools... the

power to keep silent.

When acting as a companion or advisor, the Babalon of Severity sees important aspects of her companion's true self and at the right moment, she will reveal the truth to her companion. The truth is not always attractive, and sometimes it has the power to destroy. A leader with cowardice in their heart can be helped to face their fears and benefit from its lessons, yet if they do not benefit from the mirror that Babalon creates then the time will come that she helps them to reveal it to others. This is not easy nor is it kind, yet it is necessary. Babalon ultimately passes judgement on whom is worthy of her attentions, even when those attentions may shed an ugly light on the true nature of her consort. Her own reputation is worthless to her because it is not her business what others believe. In fact she may be reviled and cast out by society, and this may even be a sign that she is being successful in her task. It is when she rises up and succeeds in providing council and secret strength that leads to social harmony, natural balance and a stable government that she is in her most balanced aspect. No claim of success can be made because she is the secret consort. She slips away in the shadows once her services are complete. Pieces fall away, down to the earth as she lays down and lets her self die. It is her only defense to be able to continue her path, and maintain her center as a timeless, endless source of strength, balance and reflection.

Her secret weapon is the knowledge of her infinite selves. She shows her consort their star, creates a reflection for them to identify themselves as a being of light. They must choose to step into this reflection because even with a perfect mirror they may choose to look away, in shame, fear, and resistance to change. Looking into the darkness of ego death is not for the faint of heart. Babalon creates and holds space for such psychic road trips.

Sometimes Babalon creates the uncomfortable reflection through force. Sexual ritual is a matrix for building safe spaces of change. Erotic

sadism enacted on the lover gives permission for them to explore what it means to be powerless. Pain and suffering when administered by a trusted secret partner can provide a release of guilt, sorrow, and regret brought on by the weight of unpleasant decisions.

It is only with supreme trust and intimacy that the ruler is able to forgive themselves and allow Babalon to externalize their shadows and slay them in the presence of the sacred Scarlet Woman. Sometimes Babalon recognizes that her consort is not experienced at causing suffering even when it is for a greater good. A strong ruler makes decisions that impact large groups of people and when some benefit, others lose. Awakening their lust and bringing about recognition of their power may be the answer to the strength of their reign. Erotically experiencing the sexual cruelty personally wreaked on Babalon may bring about the catharsis of self knowledge. Her erotic devastation tears down the walls of compassion that may bring about their death in battle. Learning not to hesitate when delivering a blow may be the difference between winning and losing the war. Finally, bringing them to the ultimate realization that pain is truly relative and a matter of perception enables them to move into their true position of divine rule. Babalon's pain is only shared with her consort when it has the intended impact to relay an experience, a reality, an alternative to their world view. She is capable of infinite transformations and shades of arousal, from terrifying inferences of harm to deep sensual strokes, she manifests the full spectrum of desire and her control of this desire is what ultimately provides the necessary influence of Change.

Seek her out whenever you see her on a street corner or on a podium. Invoke her joyfully and with lewdness under the stars for guidance and ecstatic insight. Recognize your feverish brow and frenzied movements as proof that she is here! Worship her with strange drugs and open yourself to her influence for she will open herself to you without reservation. She is timeless and her lust is shared by all. ✣

A Love Letter

by Sarah-Jayne Farrer

You have given yourself to me.
Fully. You surrendered. You're mine!
Your heart belongs to me, your soul,
Your body, your breath, your everything! Mine!
And you will run with me,
Scream with me and rut with me,
Tremble in terror and desire of me,
Dance that wild, frenzied dance with me,
Journey to the dark, dank depths with me.
And you will know sheer ecstasy, utter agony,
And the intoxicating thrill of the hunt.

And we will meet at the Crossroads together, as we always have.
We will wander far and wide, with a fire raging in your head.
And I will show you the way on those crooked and hidden paths.
I will tell you things no other could.
I will take you to places unknown, and unseen.
I will teach you. Guide you. Push you. Pull you.
Rip you open!

I will break you and remake you,
Over and over.
And you will love me.

And when I'm not with you...

Remember... Remember...

...Remember

![Chant d'Automne by Sarah-Jayne Farrer]

Chant d'Automne by Sarah-Jayne Farrer

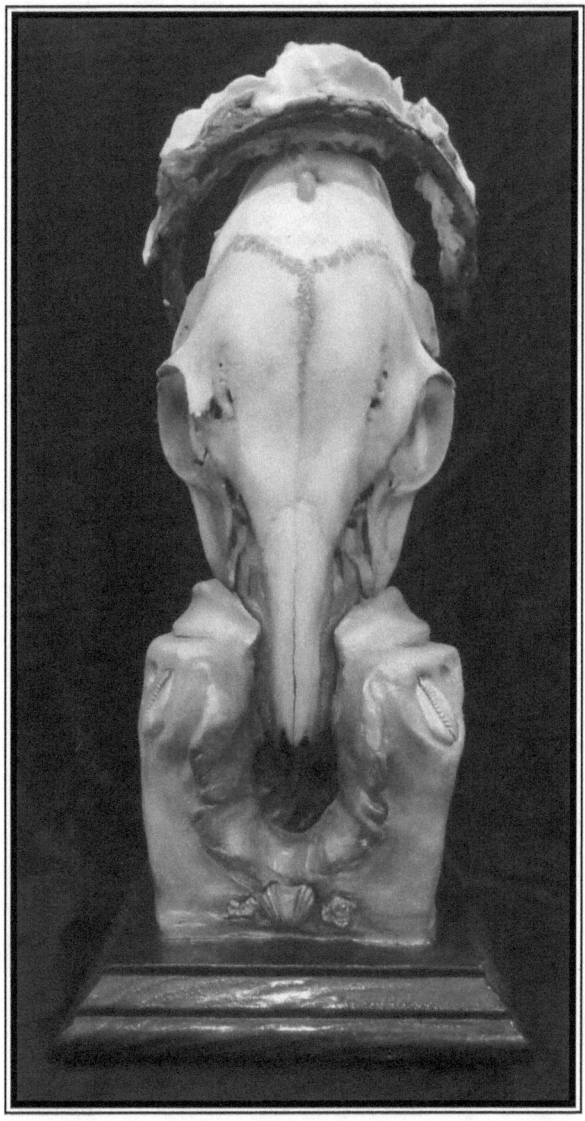

Spirit House/Womb: A Place For Things to Grow
by Mishlen Linden

Glaistig by Lorraine Sherwin

Glaistig

by Sarah-Jayne Farrer

Tri-ammonite Witch, dark transformer and blood-drenched diva beneath a baleful moon, traces petroglyphs with her hooves. Fast-flickering eyes survey her every motion, from within the ebon darkness, as she dances backwards the patterns woven in stone. Spinning in her sinister dervish through splintered walls of sleep and across the aeon-rippled tides of time, to once again emerge from forgotten shadow.

Manflesh is to be devoured.

Her copper-coated tongue sings in inhuman pitch and seductive tone; calling, luring, entrancing with swathes of green and hints of wanton, sweat-dewed skin; the accursed traveling pole, standing proud as anchor for her soul.

Flesh upon flesh. His head is lost to him now, as warm sanguine droplets fall against frigid flint whilst milk flows forth into her waiting cup to slake her thirst once more.

She exultantly shakes her crescent crowned head in the throes of forbidden desire and trusts her senses into entopic swirlings. From her cock-eyed cave she reaches towards the pinnacle, some wild, invulnerable eyrie which beckons from beyond.

She is the wilderness lost in man. ✤

Notes On Glaistig

The glaistig is a ghost from Scottish mythology, a type of fuath. It is also known as maighdean uaine (Green Maiden), and may appear as a beautiful or monstrous woman, as a half-woman half-goat similar to a faun, or in the shape of a goat. The lower goat half of her form is usually disguised by a long, flowing green robe or dress, and the woman often appears grey with long yellow hair. She is also known as "Green Jean."

The glaistig is an ambivalent ghost that appears in legend as both a malign and benign creature. Some stories have her luring men to her lair via either song or dance, where she would then drink their blood or casting stones in the path of travelers or throwing them off course.

In other, more benign incarnations, the glaistig is a type of tutelary spirit and protector of cattle and herders, and in at least one legend in Scotland, the town of Ach-na-Creige had such a spirit protecting the cattle herds. The townsfolk, in gratitude, poured milk from the cows into a hollowed-out stone for her to drink. According to the same legend, her protection was revoked after one local youth poured boiling milk into the stone, burning her. She has also been described in some folklore as watching over children while their mothers milked the cows and fathers watched over the herds.

Another rendition of the glaistig legend is that she was once a mortal noblewoman, to whom a "fairy" nature had been given or who was cursed with the goat's legs and immortality, and since has been known as "The Green Lady." She might either be benign, watching over houses and looking after the weak of mind, or appear as a vengeful ghost. In some tales she was murdered in a green dress, and then stuffed unceremoniously up the chimney by a servant. It is said that her footsteps can still be heard as she walks the castle in sadness. Such Green Lady myths have been associated with a number of locations in Scotland, including Ardnacallich, Dunollie Castle, Loch Fyne, Muchalls Castle, and in Wales at Caerphilly. A similar tale ("Ocean Born Mary") has been told in Henniker, New Hampshire.

– Excerpted from Wikipedia.org

Outro

by Lou Hotchkiss Knives

"Let her be dedicated, consecrated, blood to blood, heart to heart, mind to mind, single in will, none without the circle, all to me.
And she shall wander in the witchwood under the Night of Pan, and know the mysteries of the Goat and the Serpent, and of the children that are hidden away.
I will provide the place and the material basis, thou the tears and blood."

— Jack Parsons, *Liber 49*

This is the story of a War that is never done.

She awoke at the Dawn of Time, in the great cities of the Fertile Crescent. Magnificent and adored, she ruled from the bed of sacred harlots, in the shadow of mighty ziggurats that centuries of conflict have long since reduced to rubble.

As Christianity sought to destroy the Old Pagan World, the writings of John of Patmos named her Babylon, the Scarlet Woman, an allegory of debauched Rome in the final hours of its splendour. On the banks of the Dead Sea, Gnostics shared stories of her timeless song. Her Word was buried in the desert, her perfume still lingering, centuries later, upon the scrolls of *Thunder, Perfect Mind*.

During the Renaissance, as the hegemony of the Catholic Church collapsed and heresies and conflicts tore at the fabric of Europe, she

returned to haunt the visions of conjurer John Dee. But it was Aleister Crowley who, four centuries later, coined her sacred name, Babalon, as black clouds spread their mantle of sorrow over the horizon, announcing the impending catastrophe of War. As a terrified Humanity entered the atomic age, Jack Parsons carried her banner into the era of space travel and Individualism.

You've probably gathered, by now, that Babalon delights in Passion and Chaos alike. Historically, she seems to reveal herself to humans in times of deep collective doubt and conflict. Our rapidly changing 21st Century civilisation is one such time. All the conditions are fulfilled for Her to make her bed of harlotry once again in our midst: a capitalist system that slowly but surely chokes our planet up, a global population that continues rising despite limited resources, a digital culture which is slowly estranging the new generations from the realities of Nature, and a system of values that rewards money over poetry. Religious fanatics are everywhere, preaching their gangsta-Kalashnikov brand of enlightenment via the Internet and enforcing the worst kind of patriarchal sexual repression in the territories they control.

Everywhere, hostility and violence against women is on the rise. The rape of Mother Nature goes on as humanity disconnects itself further from the reality of the Planet's true generative and destructive potential. We are dancing on the edge of Destruction. This is why Babalon has returned.

We are the daughters of centuries of Night and Fire. In our genes we carry the untold stories of our foremothers, each one of us the heir to a motherline that never passed on its name because it never had one. Our past is a long crepuscular walk, our present is uncertain. Yet, through it all, we have always carried within us the Mysteries of Womanhood, untouched, immutable and eternal. We are the Witchcraft, a fact no amount of hatred and violence can ever eradicate. We stand at the very gates of Existence, our bodies the keys to the riddle of Life in

all its grotesque and sublime potential. We have given birth to every hero and every zero since the Dawn of Humanity. Our bodies are the most indispensable and sacred resource on this Earth, yet the most underrated. Our blood cycles are the guarantee of the survival of the species. Our Love alone decides who lives and who dies. Starved of our affection and care, infants give up on life, children wither like flowers.

Yet Death lingers within us too, anathema to those who can't see the Shadows for the Light. Our bodies act as gateways to the Underworld, and sometimes we choose to shun the sacrifices of child rearing and birth altogether, our allegiance to Chaos a disturbing blow to those who still vow a cult to traditional motherhood. Sometimes we feel our offspring die within the womb, returning to the Void that lies inside us and beyond (an experience unique to those of us who were born female). Such is the capricious dance of Existence, which is reflected in our Mysteries. Nature is not always kind to new Life. Some argue that maternal instinct may well be a construct, after all. Females of many species, like Saturn, have been known to devour their new-borns. Our culture recoils at the mere idea of the murdering mother, of the black hole that sucks everything back into Nothingness, that destroys rather than nurtures. The nightmare of the *vagina dentata* still lingers in the collective unconscious. It is from that primitive terror of being at the mercy of an omnipotent Nature that the fear of women and the oppression of women arise.

> *I have gone out, a possessed witch, haunting the*
> *black air, braver at night; dreaming evil, I have done*
> *my hitch over the plain houses, light by light: lonely*
> *thing, twelve-fingered, out of mind.*
> – Anne Sexton, *Her Kind*

We are the Women of Babalon. We live our lives on the edge, we always have. We've been to all tomorrow's parties, and we've sat through

many a sunrise. Sometimes we play with fire and get burnt, yet we understand, viscerally, that knowledge of the alchemical formula that turns lead into wild roses is a *sine qua non* on a path forever riddled with challenges and ordeals. We have many a transformational story to tell, and many teachings to share.

We are the Women of Babalon, the wanderers of Darkness and Light.

We know that wisdom lies within the flesh, and that by training our bodies, our minds, and our senses, we can access revelations of Divine Love. Where Church and State unite to condemn, regulate and repress the erotic, we break their ultimate taboo and turn sex into a sacrament.

The modern Pagan community still shies away from embracing tantric mysteries. We have spent the last years of the 20th century trying to make ourselves respectable and accepted by the mainstream. Remember the days when the gutter press was gloating over our alleged drug-fuelled pedophile Satanic Nazi orgies? Whilst we may have succeeded in dispelling many of the myths concerning our spiritual practice, our community seems to have lost a bit of its former seductive allure along the way. It is our responsibility to ensure sacred sex and sensuality remain part of the magickal landscape.

We stand for Love, Life and Divine Drunkenness.

We are the Women of Babalon. We serve Her with pride in this Age of Decay, with a degree of spiritual freedom and autonomy that was unimaginable for Western women only two hundred years ago. Through Babalon we reconnect with our once demonised bodies, rediscovering our long forgotten voices. We are also able, for the first time in centuries, to embrace the primeval rage of womanhood, the ugly, Kali-like current that reflects the wrath of Earth as a destructive

Titaness. As we've pointed out before, our goddess tends to dwell amongst us when civilisation teeters on the brink of chaos. That time is now. As Jack Parsons prophesised, women will have a part to play in the coming Apocalypse. By reconnecting ourselves with the Mysteries, we begin to heal the divide that separates us (and Mankind) from Nature. Of course, we are also aware it may well already be too late. Let us be realistic: our rituals, our magick alone will not stop wars nor will they reverse the effects of Climate Change. Yet in our spirituality lies the key to apprehend the changes ahead. Like it or not, we are all bound to the initiations of womb and tomb. Destruction, inevitably, lies at the end of each journey, but every step we take on the way has the power to sway the crowd of the dancers left or right, closer towards the stars, or further down the abyss. We can teach them the moves. We can write them songs that defy time. Like the Scottish witches of old, we can beat the seashore rocks with rags and chant spells to raise storms. Like them, we are wild and untamed; like them, we know we have nothing to lose.

So here is the proposition:

Let us Love as warriors, freely, beautifully, shamelessly, gratuitously, defiantly, relentlessly. Let us spend those transient lives of ours doing Her work, Her star high on our banners, so our Art/Hearts may be guided by Her hand, our voices become one. May we strive to turn our lives into stories to re-enchant and transform our dying World.

In this War, every heart is a revolutionary cell.

– October, 2014

En Finale

by Mishlen Linden

There may be those who look at our writings and do not see themselves reflected. No, you may not be reflected for we have all come by different paths to reach out to the Divine. You who read this, you too will find your own methods, your path into eternal ecstasy.

We are here to remind you that
YOU ARE FREE

It's heady stuff, being an incarnation of the PRIMAL SOURCE, and being worshiped in awe. Remember, you share this with every woman. We are simply being trained to use our bodies, while others have been discouraged from that very practice.

Always give freely of your time and energy to help aspirants as they search as you once did for the Power that lies inside each of Us.

The office of the Scarlet Woman demands love and respect and it is for the priest to give that love and respect. But that very office of the Scarlet Woman also demands the same of YOU.

Take delight in All-of-Us

Take all with humility, and in honor, walk that path, hand-in-hand.

Biographies

Sharmon Davidson-Jennings

Sharmon Davidson-Jennings began her artistic career as a graphic designer, and then chose to put her career on hold, devoting several years to raising her children. During this time, she earned a BFA in Drawing and a BA in Art Education from Northern Kentucky University, performed in a Middle Eastern dance troupe, and educated herself in a wide variety of spiritual traditions ranging from Thelemic magick to Wicca to Native American shamanism. She has been a follower of Tibetan Buddhism for the last fifteen years.

In addition, she has taught in the Kentucky public schools, furthered her education at the prestigious Art Academy of Cincinnati, and completed a Master's degree. Exhibiting professionally since 1994, she has won awards in both regional and national juried exhibitions, and her art has been featured in several magazines and on book covers. Davidson was selected for inclusion in Art Buzz: The 2014 Collection, a premier showcase for an eclectic collection of top quality, contemporary visual art from around the world. She is currently represented by the Promenade Gallery in Berea, Kentucky, and is a member of the Kentucky Guild of Artists and Craftsmen.

Davidson's work originates from a deep belief in the sanctity of nature, and in the unity of every particle in our universe. Formed from common elements born from a common source, everything is interconnected in the most intricate ways, both visible and invisible. Over time, she has developed a vocabulary of personal symbols

through which she attempts to express this idea. Each piece develops organically and intuitively, as layers of transparent color along with other materials are built up. Time and personal experience have also become important ingredients for revealing this mystery.

To see more of her work, view her website at: www.sharmondavidson.com

Emma Doeve

My first impulse when it comes to creative self-expression is visual. The world I was born into, (which is now Indonesia), and left long before I became fully conscious–is a lush tropical one. It's a world invisible to me here now in the West. I've always sensed it is a female world, even though its religion is predominantly Muslim. It was under colonial rule for 350 years. You can go to some parts of the planet and experience an absence of liberties (especially female) that we take for granted here.

I have no huge solidarity with it–in the sense that I would want to go out there and engage with it, politically or socially–but it gives me a double awareness and a very personal sentience of gender, and particularly our relationship to Nature where it all starts.

For a further look at the visual work of Emma Doeve, plus background information and contact details, please go to whollybooks.wordpress.com/emma-doeve.

Lilith Dorsey, M.A.

Lilith Dorsey, M.A., hails from many magickal traditions, including Celtic, Afro-Caribbean, and Native American spirituality. Her traditional education focused on Plant Science, Anthropology, and Film at the University of RI, New York University and the University

of London. Her magickal training includes numerous initiations in Santeria also known as Lucumi, Haitian Vodoun, and New Orleans Voodoo.

Lilith is a Voodoo Priestess and in that capacity has been doing successful magick since 1991 for patrons, is editor/publisher of *Oshun-African Magickal Quarterly*, filmmaker of the experimental documentary *Bodies of Water: Voodoo Identity and Tranceformation*, author of *Voodoo and Afro-Caribbean Paganism*, and *The African-American Ritual Cookbook, 55 Ways to Connect to Goddess*, and choreographer for the jazz legend Dr. John's "Night Tripper" Voodoo Show.

Facebook: www.facebook.com/groups/lilithdorsey

Linda Falorio

Linda Falorio is an internationally recognized artist and writer, and creator of the Occult bestseller, *The Shadow Tarot*. First published in 1988, *The Shadow Tarot* was created as an exploration tool for delving into those areas of the psyche that find their reflection in the Collective Unconscious and the Archetypal Shadow. These images reflect the "nightside" of consciousness as opposed to our ordinary "dayside" reality. The newly released and much anticipated edition of *The Shadow Tarot* includes full color images of all seventy-eight cards as inspired by Aleister Crowley's *Liber 231*, Kenneth Grant's *The Nightside Of Eden*, and *The Lesser Key of Solomon: Goetia*. Linda is also known for her magickal altarpieces, magickal portraits and for interpreting personal symbols and dreams on canvas.

Translated into six languages, Linda's work has been featured in books and magazines and includes *Lost Souls*, a collection of her own short stories with a magickal twist, soon to be reissued, contributions to

Faces of Babalon, with Mishlen Linden, *Thee Kali Circle Compendium*, with Topy Heart, *Starfire Magazine, Skoob Occult Review, Tarot Network News, Modern Sex Magick*, by Donald Michael Kraig, *NOXAZ Sirius Anthology 2014*, edited by Edgar Kerval and many others.

Linda says of herself: "I seek through the spark of Art to delight and to inspire, to mold Archetypes of human consciousness into new and visionary forms, to evolve new Goddesses and Gods, to invent new dreams and reach for Utopian Magicks that together we may yet create." Kenneth Grant said of her: "[Linda is] indeed a High Priestess of Typhon—and a methodical one at that!" Linda holds advanced degrees in psychology and psychotherapy and has utilized and taught astrology, tarot, palmistry, hypnotherapy, magick and meditation in her clinical practice.

For more information, please visit Linda's websites: www.anandazone.nu and www.shadowtarot.net

SARAH-JAYNE FARRER

As far back as she can recall, Sarah-Jayne Farrer has lived and breathed the Arte Magical. Her vision and voice carry the pure essence of rustic wisdom and the twisted cold logic of dark faerie tale. Her English roots are woven and knotted into the ancient landscape she wanders through, her Sorcerous ways are nightborne and heavily sensual. With no uncertainty, Queen Lillith and Lady Babalon have called and guided her across the thresholds to gush out their power into this pale and embittered world. You may find Sarah-Jayne's work gracing the pages of Lodge Horus Maat's *Silver Star Journal of New Magick* and *Hoofprints in the Wildwood* (a devotional anthology for the Horned God in all of his manifestations) but primarily in the gloom laden mystique of inthechimehours.com, Sarah-Jayne's enigmatic website.

Lou Hotchkiss Knives

Lou Hotchkiss Knives (née Louise Lisse) was born in Northern France and grew up immersed in Greek myths and French classical literature which drew heavily on Greek and Roman authors. A self-declared pagan from the age of seven, she spent her childhood longing for the return of a goddess-based pagan faith, doing little rituals in her room and dreaming of a spiritual new homeland across the sea .

At 23, after a degree in English, she moved to England where she took the plunge, finally met with other occultists and became initiated in a ritual magick circle. After further studies in Education, she got involved in teaching Magick to newcomers at her local moot, helped organise talks at pagan events, and became involved in women's issues via her involvement in the local punk scene. She became a devotee of Babalon in 2008 after reading Peter Grey's book *The Red Goddess*.

In 2011 she started writing articles for local pagan magazines and doing talks on History and pagan practice at local occult events. Her spirituality encompasses her ritual and ecstatic practices, her dreaming and love life and is channelled through writing, poetry and live music performance.

She currently lives in Devon, England where she shares her time between her work in education, writing and performing. This is her first full-length published occult work.

Facebook: www.facebook.com/The.French.machine.gun
www.reverbnation.com/husbandsnknives

Ayahna Kumarroy

I don't know where all of this began…I have been living this life with the spirits for as long as I can remember. At some point I began creating, "making" Art. Art is a way for me to understand these mysteries, to

decipher the language and dialogue all around and surrounding "me." I spend most of my time here in service and devotion to Mother in her multifaceted appearances, and with the Dead, and ever more so among the forgotten and unheard Dead.

Facebook: www.facebook.com/ayahna.kumarroy

GERALDINE LAMBERT

Geraldine Lambert lives in the south of England and studied Graphics and Fine Art (with a particular interest in pictorial imagery) at the University of Portsmouth. She taught Art and Typography for many years before pursuing her path as an artist within the genre of the occult and esoteric.

Describing herself as a 'hedge-rider' and magician (she is a member of the Order of the Morning Star) she illustrates the visions that come from creative interplay when worlds collide, bringing in their wake sublime magical communication. Her predominant use of inks and oil paint, together with techniques employed in her wood-engraved prints, gives rise to a recognisable style using line and movement as signatures of her work.

Her paintings and prints have been published and exhibited in shows throughout the UK and can be viewed on her website:
www.geraldine-lambert.net

MADELEINE LEDESPENCER

Madeleine Ledespencer is a visual artist and author born and raised in the Southern United States. Madeleine travels extensively for her art and writing – from Europe, to South America, to the Antipodes. Her work often focuses on themes of transmutation and transformation,

drawing from diverse sources such as the Grimoire tradition, Traditional Witchcraft, as well as direct spirit communications and mediumship.

She has written on contemporary occultism as well as the occultists of the French Decadence. In addition to her own writing and art, Madeleine also works with the *Abraxas* journal out of London curating artists and authors for publication.

She can be reached via email at eindoppelganger@gmail.com.

Mishlen Linden

We are the Dreamers, and we are the Dream.

I include intimate details from my Magickal Record in my manuscript because life and magick is intimate and lives in the present. Whatever I have done, you can do. Whatever I have attained you can certainly go beyond. I and the community of women want to learn from your work and experiments. You are everything I have ever hoped to be. Shine Brightly!

I believe that it is depth of experience that makes good art, not only technique. As a Babalon, we search for experiences that feed our work. Our art is talismanic, carrying the power of the force which created it. Our journey is an inward one. We walk upon the shores of the underworld and bring up our mental snapshots to share with the world. My children are borne of the cast-off shells of life–bone, stone, and deadwood, brought back to life again. They are for those who see their value.

Art is my life. Magick is the way in which I live my life. Icons, sculptures and paintings are my children. They are wild and free. I have been told that it is best not to get in front of me when I am driving. All else is rather inconsequential.

As to labels, Thelemic Tibetan Buddhist will do. My work can be

seen at mishlenlinden.com I am the author of *Typhonian Teratomas: The Shadows of the Abyss,* and editor of and contributor to *Faces of Babalon,* both published by Black Moon Publishing. I can be reached at: mishlenlinden@gmail.com

Maegdlyn Morris

Maegdlyn is a magician that as archivist for Black Moon, preserves the secrets, and experimental rituals of generations of necromancers, chaotes and madmen/women. She is a presenter and counselor on such topics as LHP, sex magick, polyamory, and the future of American neopaganism. She has worked with Louis Martinié in researching Dr. John's history, and worked rituals at Babalon Rising and Starwood to open the way. Her work with Babalon permeates every relationship, and dictates the path that she illuminates. She currently resides in a magic cabin in the woods with her husband, partner, and many rude creatures of habit, producing artwork and music. She may be contacted at maegdlyn@gmail.com.

Dianne Mystérieux

Dianne was last seen circa '73 riding away from the Horus Maat Abbey on the back of a motor-cycle with an unknown driver. The painting on page 120 by her with her image as Babalon and a few memories remain accessible.

Diane Narraway

Diane Narraway comes from an occult background that focused on both science and mystery and has herself practised magick in a variety

of forms from a very young age.

She is both a mother and grandmother which she embraces with the same enthusiasm as her role as chairperson and one of the ceremonial facilitators of The Dolmen Grove (a large multipath spiritual organisation), as well as editor of their fast growing online publication, *Dolmen Grove Chronicles*.

As a magickian she incorporates both the archaic and the contemporary in her ritual workings. Her own path and spiritual development often sees her at the fore-front of the pagan and occult world where she regularly talks on magick and divination. Her public work focuses upon the creation of new traditions that will lay the foundations for future generations to build upon.

As a writer she has written many articles on a variety of subjects of interest to both the magickal and the pagan community as well as short stories, poetry and rituals.

She can be reached at www.facebook.com/diane.narraway
www.facebook.com/DolmenGroveMagazine
email: dolmengrove@dolmengrove.co.uk

Charlotte Rodgers

Charlotte Rodgers is an animist whose life is lived around the creative magickal act in its myriad of manifestations.

After a peripheral existence and chaotic life travelling through Australasia and Europe, she eventually settled in Somerset, England.

She is initiated into the AMOOKOS and Uttara Kaula Tantric traditions and has done long-term Setian and Nightside work, but has presently stopped all group practice in favour of solitary explorations.

Charlotte co-founded the Omphalos Group, organised magickal art, music and film events and created sculptures from remnants of death.

She has had many articles published and is the author of *P is for*

Prostitution; A Modern Primer' 'The Bloody Sacrifice' and 'The Sky is a Gateway not a Ceiling'. Charlotte also conceived, introduced and co-edited *'A Contemporary Western Book of the Dead'*.
www.perdurabu.com

Lorraine Sherwin

Lorraine's background is in natural paganism, magick and the occult –'a child of the woods,' close to Dionysus. Magick and sexual magick were of immediate interest and became lifelong passions.

Amongst others, Aleister Crowley and Austin Osman Spare have been major influences in thought, deed and art.

Experienced in group ritual Lorraine proffers a solitary path here. Babalon inevitably finds her way into Lorraine's paintings, drawings and dances.

An artist and oriental dancer, Lorraine's interests progressed, along with husband, chaos magician Ray Sherwin, into body-working techniques of various types–further springboards into an energetic form of self-discovery and transformation.

She lives in Fuerteventura with Ray and their daughter.
Facebook: www.facebook.com/lorraine.sherwin

Semirani Vine

A lust to express experience through the visual image has lead Semirani 'Sem' Vine many places, an absorption in its practice both a removal from and an immersion in this fascinating world and in fascinating worlds. For many years wonderful opportunities and a passion for art and history, the story of humankind, meant varied work as a resident artist and illustrator for many Dorset museums and being involved in academic studies, taking private commissions as

well as exploring and exhibiting personal art development in diverse mediums including the written word, with an emphasis on time and movement. Over the last eight years, Sem has moved into newer ways of working, using both physically and metaphysically diverse materials as motivation demands, provoked by a hypersensitivity to spontaneous and emotive response free from an emphasis on a concrete end product. This philosophy is thus fed into an informative way of being, study and direction, and also richly informs the artwork and design that she continues to produce, including work for heritage based projects, for the medieval Celtic rock band, The Dolmen and as part of the miscellany of united spirits that are the Dolmen Grove.

For further information, feel free to contact her at hi@semvine.com.

Women of Babalon Group

Portal
Communication & Community
An Open Forum

All are invited to join us on the official Facebook page of the Women of Babalon!

Share your thoughts, dreams and experiences.
Find out more about Babalon and sacred sexuality

Contact the authors or artists

Discuss the issues raised on the page with other readers and like-minded people

We are a supportive community of women sharing our beginnings and our present magicks, thoughts, and experiences. Those new to Babalon, those experienced in the current are all welcome. We extend a special invitation and seek to be particularly helpful to those who have just discovered Babalon. Men with whom we share interests are welcome to join us.

The roller coaster that is Babalon is common to all of us. We invite each and every one of you to join us for the ride.

There is a community out there waiting for your input. Come and help us spread the Word...

WomenofBabalon.com
or
Facebook: In your Facebook searchbar simply type:
Women of Babalon – Community

Nuit by Mishlen Linden

Other Publications by
BLACK MOON PUBLISHING

~ THE FACES OF BABALON ~
A COMPILATION OF WOMEN'S VOICES
by Mishlen Linden, Linda Falorio, Soror Chen, Nema
and Raven Greywalker

~ TYPHONIAN TERATOMAS: THE SHADOWS OF THE ABYSS ~
by Mishlen Linden

~ WATERS OF RETURN: THE AEONIC FLOW OF VOUDOO ~
by Louis Martinié

~ A PRIEST'S HEAD, A DRUMMER'S HANDS ~
NEW ORLEANS VOODOO ORDER OF SERVICE
by Louis Martinié

~ TALKING TO GOD WITH FOOD: QUESTIONING ANIMAL SACRIFICE ~
by Louis Martinié

~ DR. JOHN MONTANEE: A GRIMOIRE ~
by Dr. Louie Martinié

~ THE PRIESTHOOD: PARAMETERS AND RESPONSIBILITIES by Nema ~

~ MAATIAN MEDITATIONS AND CONSIDERATIONS ~
A CONTINUATION OF PAST WRITINGS ON "SHE WHO MOVES"
by Nema

~ FEATHER AND FIRESNAKE by Nema ~

~ Wings of Rapture by Nema ~

~ Enochian Temples by Benjamin Rowe ~

~ The Book of the Seniors by Benjamin Rowe ~

~ The 91 Parts of the Earth by Benjamin Rowe ~

~ Lucifer: The Light of The New Aeon ~
Edited by Diane Narraway
Featuring contributions by:
Orlee Andromedae, Teach Carter, Jaclyn Cherie,
Linda Cunningham, James Ford, Isis Graywood,
Elizabeth Jennings, Amanda Lindupp, Rachel Summers,
Geraldine Lambert, Maxim, Eirwen Morgan,
Diane Narraway, Richard K. Page, Laurie Pneumatikos,
Cheryl Waldron, and Sean Witt
and cover art by Matt Baldwin-Ives.

~ Songs of The Black Flame ~
by Diane Narraway

~ The Occult Digest ~
A Journal of Esoteric Thought, Practice and Expression
Edited by Louis Martinié

BLACKMOONPUBLISHING.COM

WOMEN OF BABALON:
A HOWLING OF WOMEN'S VOICES

This is a book of sexual magicks in both theory and practice from the feminine power zones and from their own points of view. Very little has been written on this. It is a compilation composed of the text and art of sixteen practicing female magickians through which the vital character of a Babalon is explored.

Both the elder and younger Babalons write here in order to expand upon this almost taboo subject. Linda Falorio, one of the writers within, says "Men, read on if you want to know our deepest secrets."

This book focuses on the 'what,' the 'who' and the 'how' of the practice.

The materials are mutli-generational, multi-cultural and multi-systematic, though with a strong emphasis on Thelemic.

No 'right' way is posited. Often seen 'shoulds' are replaced by an ethic that values Choice.

Being a Babalon is both a spiritual and social challenge. There are no more optimal conditions outside of an open heart and mind. She is much more than any sexual orientation or specific sexual act.

Although there is no definitive word or image which captures the totality of what it means to be a Babalon, her very nature speaks to Change. Babalon spins and the walls between worlds revolve. Her spinning gives form to the very womb of life. She rides upon a crest that peeks into the heavens, and descends into the very heart of hell.

The papers and images in this book document this journey, and the howling of women will now make itself heard!

www.ingramcontent.com/pod-product-compliance
Lightning Source LLC
Chambersburg PA
CBHW030855170426
43193CB00009BA/624